D0207683

LATINO AMERICAN FOLKTALES

Recent Titles in
Stories from the American Mosaic

Native American Folktales
Thomas A. Green

African American Folktales
Thomas A. Green

LATINO AMERICAN FOLKTALES

Edited by
Thomas A. Green

Stories from the American Mosaic

GREENWOOD PRESS
Westport, Connecticut • London

Library of Congress Cataloging-in-Publication Data

Latino American folktales / edited by Thomas A. Green
    p. cm. — (Stories from the American mosaic)
  Includes bibliographical references and index.
  ISBN 978–0–313–36299–6 (alk. paper)
1. Latin Americans—Folklore. 2. Tales—Latin America. I. Green, Thomas A., 1944–
GR114.L37   2009
398.208968'073—dc22   2008040216

British Library Cataloguing in Publication Data is available.

Copyright © 2009 by Thomas A. Green

All rights reserved. No portion of this book may be
reproduced, by any process or technique, without the
express written consent of the publisher.

Library of Congress Catalog Card Number: 2008040216
ISBN: 978–0–313–36299–6

First published in 2009

Greenwood Press, 88 Post Road West, Westport, CT 06881
An imprint of Greenwood Publishing Group, Inc.
www.greenwood.com

Printed in the United States of America

The paper used in this book complies with the
Permanent Paper Standard issued by the National
Information Standards Organization (Z39.48-1984).

10 9 8 7 6 5 4 3 2 1

Contents

Preface   vii

Origins   1

  Quetzalcoatl and Tezcatlipoca   3

  Jesus   7

  The Peak of Gold   11

  Becoming American   17

Heroes, Heroines, Villains, and Fools   21

  The Little Green Rabbit   23

  A New Mexico David   28

  John Tiger   34

  The Boy Who Became a King   39

  Maria the Ash Girl   45

  Blanca Flor   48

  The Bear Prince   52

  The Prohibited Chamber   57

  Tale of the Rabbit   59

  Brother Coyote   67

  Sister Fox and Brother Coyote   70

  Pedro de Urdemalas   75

  Pablo Apodaca and the Bear   80

Society and Conflict   85

  Manuel Jesus Vasques: A Life on the Southwest Frontier   87

  Francisco Trujillo and Billy the Kid   91

Elfego Baca   99

Sunday Seven   104

The Bird of the Sweet Song   108

The Louse Skin Coat   111

The Supernatural   113

Princess Papantzin's Resurrection   115

Clemencia and José   118

The Giant's Secret   121

La Llorona   124

Bullet-Swallower   127

The Accursed Bell   133

El Señor Milagroso Rescues a Stingy Son   139

The Penitent Brothers   141

The Living Spectre   150

Three Live Witches   155

The Witch Deer   160

Witch Tales from New Mexico   165

Select Bibliography   169

Index   171

Preface

Latino American Folktales is designed to provide educators, students, and general readers with examples of a range of traditional Latino narrative types: fictional tales, legends, myths, and personal experience narratives. Moreover, the examples in this anthology represent the cultural diversity within the American Latino. Native North, Central, and South American influences are apparent in the Latino repertoire by virtue of the inclusion of characters such as Coyote and Tigre (Jaguar) in fictional tales, and by the incorporation of Native American historical figures such as Montezuma and Papantzin into the legend corpus.

With the entry of Alvar Nunez Cabeza de Vaca into the Southwestern Region (1528), Spanish culture began to shape the lore of what eventually became New Spain, later Mexico, and still later the states of Texas, New Mexico, Arizona, and neighboring states. After his travels through Texas and New Mexico, Cabeza de Vaca returned to Spain with the stories of vast riches (see "The Peak of Gold") that encouraged increased Spanish exploration and settlement in the Americas. With the Spanish came both European folklore and Roman Catholicism. Individually and in combination with Native American perceptions of the supernatural, belief tales, personal experience narratives, and legends such as "Jesus," "The Penitent Brothers," and "Clemencia and José" reveal a potent mix of religion and magic, mysticism and medicine.

Into the twenty-first century, the Latino folktale repertoire continues to be enriched by infusions from Mexico, Central and South America, and the Caribbean. These tales reflect the environment, cultural adaptations, and prevailing concerns of the respective areas from which they are drawn. The introductions to each tale comment on these issues. The concluding general bibliography provides additional resources for those readers who wish to explore these issues in greater depth.

The collection is divided into four sections. "Origins" encompasses those narratives that focus on beginnings and transformations: the creation of the world and its inhabitants, how animal species acquired their physical characteristics, and how the family came to be here, for example. "Heroes, Heroines, Villains, and Fools" presents a cross-section of major character types that populate Latino folktales. "Society and Conflict" contains considerations of social issues ranging from conventional morality to intergroup conflicts. Finally, "The Supernatural" concentrates on traditional tales of the dead, the magical, and the monstrous.

Most of the narratives have been modified from their original forms for the benefit of contemporary readers. The modifications have been held to the minimum necessary to translate these tales for their intended audiences, to eliminate redundancy in some cases, and, in a few cases, alternative terminology has been substituted for terms (particularly racially charged terms) that would prove offensive to contemporary readers. The source of each selection is noted at its conclusion for the benefit of readers who wish to read the original texts.

ORIGINS

Quetzalcoatl and Tezcatlipoca

The Nahua are a cluster of culturally and linguistically related groups indigenous to Mexico and Central America. Historically the Aztec are the best known of the Nahua cultures, and during the pre-Columbian era developed an advanced civilization in the area of contemporary Mexico. According to Nahua tradition they originated in Aztlan later migrating into the Mexican Plateau region. Aztlan, especially the idea of "rebuilding Aztlan," has been used as a symbol for the Brown Power movement among Chicano activists in the United States. The following myth illustrates the basic features of the sacred history upon which contemporary groups draw.

In the days of Quetzalcoatl there was abundance of everything necessary for subsistence. The maize was plentiful, the calabashes were as thick as one's arm, and cotton grew in all colors without having to be dyed. A variety of birds of rich plumage filled the air with their songs, and gold, silver, and precious stones were abundant. In the reign of Quetzalcoatl there was peace and plenty for all men.

But this blissful state was too fortunate, too happy to endure. Envious of the calm enjoyment of the god and his people the Toltecs, three wicked "necromancers"—Huitzilopochtli, Titlacahuan (or Tezcatlipoca), and Tlacahuepan—plotted their downfall. These laid evil enchantments upon the city of Tollan, and Tezcatlipoca in particular took the lead in these envious conspiracies. Disguised as an aged man with white hair, he presented himself at the palace of Quetzalcoatl, where he said to the pages-in-waiting: "Pray present me to your master the king I desire to speak with him."

The pages advised him to retire, as Quetzalcoatl was indisposed and could see no one. He requested them, however, to tell the god that he was waiting outside. They did so, and procured his admittance.

On entering the chamber of Quetzalcoatl the wily Tezcatlipoca simulated much sympathy with the suffering god-king. "How are you, my son?" he asked. "I have brought you a drug which you should drink, and which will put an end to the course of your malady."

"You are welcome, old man," replied Quetzalcoatl. "I have known for many days that you would come. I am exceedingly indisposed. The malady affects my entire system, and I can use neither my hands nor feet."

Tezcatlipoca assured him that if he partook of the medicine which he had brought him he would immediately experience a great improvement in health. Quetzalcoatl drank the potion, and at once felt much revived. The cunning Tezcatlipoca pressed another and still another cup of the potion upon him, and as it was nothing but pulque, the wine of the country, he speedily became intoxicated, and was as wax in the hands of his adversary.

Tezcatlipoca, in pursuance of his policy inimical to the Toltec state, took the form of an Indian of the name of Toueyo (Toveyo), and bent his steps to the palace of Uemac, chief of the Toltecs in temporal matters. This worthy had a daughter so fair that she was desired in marriage by many of the Toltecs, but all to no purpose, as her father refused her hand to one and all. The princess, beholding the false Toueyo passing her father's palace, fell deeply in love with him, and so tumultuous was her passion that she became seriously ill because of her longing for him. Uemac, hearing of her indisposition, bent his steps to her apartments, and inquired of her women the cause of her illness. They told him that it was occasioned by the sudden passion which had seized her for the Indian who had recently come that way. Uemac at once gave orders for the arrest of Toueyo, and he was hauled before the temporal chief of Tollan.

"Whence come you?" inquired Uemac of his prisoner, who was very scantily attired.

"Lord, I am a stranger, and I have come to these parts to sell green paint," replied Tezcatlipoca.

"Why are you dressed in this fashion? Why do you not wear a cloak?" asked the chief.

"My lord, I follow the custom of my country," replied Tezcatlipoca.

"You have inspired a passion in the breast of my daughter," said Uemac. "What should be done to you for thus disgracing me?"

"Slay me; I care not," said the cunning Tezcatlipoca.

"Nay," replied Uemac, "for if I slay you my daughter will perish. Go to her and say that she may wed you and be happy."

Now the marriage of Toueyo, to the daughter of Uemac aroused much discontent among the Toltecs; and they murmured among themselves, and said: "Wherefore did Uemac give his daughter to this Toueyo?" Uemac, having got wind of these murmurings, resolved to distract the attention of the Toltecs by making war upon the neighboring state of Coatepec.

The Toltecs assembled an armed for the fray, and having arrived at the country of the men of Coatepec, they placed Toueyo in ambush with his body-servants, hoping that he would be slain by their adversaries. But Toueyo and his men killed a large number of the enemy and put them to flight. His triumph was celebrated by Uemac with much pomp. The knightly plumes were placed upon his head, and his body was painted with red and yellow, an honour reserved for those who distinguished themselves in battle.

Tezcatlipoca's next step was to announce a great feast in Tollan, to which all the people for miles around were invited. Great crowds assembled, and danced and sang in the city to the sound of the drum. Tezcatlipoca sang to them and forced them to accompany the rhythm of his song with their feet. Faster and faster the people danced, until the pace became so furious that they were driven to madness, lost their footing, and tumbled pell-mell down a deep ravine, where they were changed into rocks. Others in attempting to cross a stone bridge precipitated themselves into the water below, and were changed into stones.

On another occasion Tezcatlipoca presented himself as a valiant warrior named Tequiua, and invited all the inhabitants of Tollan and its environs to come to the flower-garden called Xochitla. When assembled there he attacked them with a hoe, and slew a great number, and others in panic crushed their comrades to death.

Tezcatlipoca and Tlacahuepan on another occasion repaired to the marketplace of Tollan, the former displaying upon the palm of his hand a small infant whom he caused to dance and to cut the most amusing capers. This infant was in reality Huitzilopochdi, the Nahua god of war. At this sight the Toltecs crowded upon one another for the purpose of getting a better view, and their eagerness resulted in many being crushed to death. So enraged were the Toltecs at this that upon the advice of Tlacahuepan they slew both Tezcatlipoca and Huitzilopochtli. When this had been done the bodies of the slain gods gave forth such a pernicious effluvia that thousands the Toltecs died of the pestilence. The god Tlacahuepan then advised them to cast out the bodies lest worse befell them, but on their attempting to do so they discovered their weight to be so great that they could not move them. Hundreds wound cords round the corpses, but the strands broke, and those who pulled upon them fell and died suddenly, tumbling one upon the other, and suffocating those upon whom they collapsed.

The Toltecs were so tormented by the enchantments of Tezcatlipoca that it was soon apparent to them that their fortunes were on the wane and that the end of their empire was at hand. Quetzalcoatl, chagrined at the turn things had taken, resolved to quit Tollan and go to the country of Tlapallan, whence he had come on his civilizing mission to Mexico. He burned all the houses which he had built, and buried his treasure of gold and precious stones in the deep valleys between the mountains. He changed the cacao-trees into mesquites, and he ordered all the birds of rich plumage and song to quit the valley of Anahuac and to follow him to a distance of more than a hundred leagues.

On the road from Tollan he discovered a great tree at a point called Quauhtitlan. There he rested, and requested his pages to hand him a mirror. Regarding himself in the polished surface, he exclaimed, "I am old," and from that circumstance the spot was named Huehuequauhtitlan (Old Quauhtitlan). Proceeding on his way accompanied by musicians who played the flute, he walked until fatigue arrested his steps, and he seated himself upon a stone, on which he left the imprint of his hands. This place is called Temacpalco (The Impress of the Hands). At Coaapan he was met by the Nahua gods [the necromancers Huitzilopochtli, Tezcatlipoca, and Tlacahuepan, who were inimical to him and to the Toltecs].

"Where do you go?" they asked him. "Why do you leave your capital?"

"I go to Tlapallan," replied Quetzalcoatl, "whence I came."

"For what reason?" persisted the enchanters.

"My father the Sun has called me thence," replied Quetzalcoatl.

"Go, then, happily," they said, "but leave us the secret of your art, the secret of founding in silver, of working in precious stones and woods, of painting, and of feather-working, and other matters."

But Quetzalcoatl refused, and cast all his treasures into the fountain of Cozcaapa (Water of Precious Stones). At Cochtan he was met by another enchanter, who asked him whither he was bound, and on learning his destination proffered him a draught of wine. On tasting the vintage Quetzalcoatl was overcome with sleep.

Continuing his journey in the morning, the god passed between a volcano and the Sierra Nevada (Mountain of Snow), where all the pages who accompanied him died of cold. He regretted this misfortune exceedingly, and wept, lamenting their fate with most bitter tears and mournful songs. On reaching the summit of Mount Poyauhtecatl he slid to the base. Arriving at the seashore, he embarked upon a raft of serpents, and was wafted away toward the land of Tlapallan.

Source: Adapted from "Myths of Quetzalcoatl and Tezcatlipoca," Lewis Spence. *The Myths of Mexico and Peru* (London: G. G. Harrap and Company, 1913), pp. 60–65.

Jesus

In the following myth Native Central American and Christian European beliefs are combined to create an image of Jesus in which he is both creator of and culture hero (bringer of civilization) for humanity. The anti-Semitism apparent in the tale is likely to be a heritage of 16th century Spanish rather than any deeply held sentiments of the group that adopted and adapted Christian sacred narrative to its own purposes.

Jesus Christ was born in the night in Jerusalem, as we know. San Jose and the Virgin Maria were his parents. They were merchants, and they traveled together. They asked many rich people to let them stay in their houses, but the people refused because they thought Jose and Maria were thieves.

Eventually, they came to the house of one rich man and asked to stay in their house. They were told that they could not remain there, but they could, if they wished, stay in a stable where the sheep, cows and other animals were kept with their herders. So they went there.

At about 3 A.M., or a little later, when the star Santiago came out, Maria gave birth to a boy with stars on his palms and forehead and who lighted up the world. All of the herders came to see the child, and immediately the owner (patron) of the house came.

That night it snowed very hard and the child was very cold, so that it stiffened as if dead. The herders ran for the animals; and the sheep and the cows breathed onto the child's body and warmed it, and the child revived.

Itinerant peddlers are common in Guatemala. It is local custom to seek shelter in private homes. Thus this part of the story is familiar.

Then Jesus blessed these animals; but the horses and mules, when they had come, had not believed that the child was God and instead of breathing on him they had belched at him. God was angry with these animals and said that they would never be eaten by man, but would have to be beasts of burden always.

Christ preached to all the people who wished to listen, but some were bad and would not hear him. He wandered around and visited 5,000 pueblos and 5,000 churches, and 5,000 gardens all over the world. When he encountered a blind man on the road, he told him he would be cured the next day, and the man would be cured; when he met a deaf man, he would tell him that he would hear the next day, and the man would hear.

The Jews were very angry when Christ preached to the people, and they took him to a penitentiary of pure stone and imprisoned him in a dungeon without light or water. God [Jesus] left his cell, and when the Jews would look in to see if he was still there they saw the light of a firefly, in the dark place, and they thought Jesus was sitting there smoking a cigarette.

After 20 days, they no longer saw the firefly, so they thought Jesus was dead. Now Jesus changed the penitentiary into a large church with altars, pine-needles, flowers, tables, candles, incense, and saints' images. And when the Jews went to the penitentiary to see if Jesus was dead, they saw the church. Maybe this was the first church in the world. The Jews wondered "What are all these things," and were angry and went out to look for Jesus so they could capture him again.

There was a small road in the mountains and God was running on it with the Jews in pursuit when he saw a woman in a house off the road. He asked if he could come in, and the woman said, "With much pleasure" and admitted him. The Jews were coming quickly, and Jesus hurried into the house. There were some chicken eggs in the house and God told the woman he would bless them. He did so, and instantly the eggs were young chickens. He then went outside, where he saw a ramos plant (a grass) and he hid behind the plant; the grass covered him over, so when the Jews came up they could not see him.

The Jews came up and asked the woman where Jesus was, saying that they knew that he had passed that way. The woman said that he had passed there 20 days before (arguing to herself that the chickens could not have grown so big in less than 20 days). The Jews passed on rapidly.

Then Jesus came from hiding and went again on the road. The Jews came back, and when Jesus saw that they were upon him, he climbed a tree. The Jews had the custom of always looking at the ground: they could not look straight ahead or upward; so they did not see Jesus in the tree. But they saw his shadow, and beat it with a stick until they thought they had killed him. Then they passed on.

Jesus came down from the tree and lay down in its shade. Then he blessed the tree that it should serve for cacao. Instantly there was cacao. He told the people (the good Jews who were his followers) that the cacao should serve in *cofradias* [organizations in charge of caring for saints' images and holding their festivals], in marriages, and for borrowing money and maize [offering cacao beans is a formal way of requesting a loan]. Then the Virgin Maria came up to him, and because Jesus was thirsty she gave him some water in a glass. God blessed the water and it changed into liquor, so that it should serve later for *cofradias,* marriages, and borrowing money and maize. Then Maria went away.

Jesus began his wanderings, through the towns and mountains, again. The Jews finally found him and put him in the penitentiary. Then they took him from prison and took him to the mountains to make a cross. They came to a large tree from which to make the cross. The Jews began to try to chop the tree down with their axes; but each chip that flew away fell into a spring and became a snake (which attacked the feet of the Jews) or a frog, or a toad. These were bad signs for the Jews, and they said that Jesus would not die then. They then asked Jesus to cut the tree himself, and he agreed to do so. With one blow of the ax a chip came off and fell in the water and became a fish (This is why we eat fish during Holy Week). The next chip became a quetzal [a type of tropical bird], a very large one. The next became a large chicken. With each subsequent chip came another food animal.

The tree was finally felled by Jesus, and the Jews made a cross. Jesus had to drag the cross to another place. They stopped on the way to eat. The Jews wrung the neck of the chicken and put it in a pot to cook. They cut off the feet and the wings and they had pure meat, and then they put the chicken in a large leaf with much pepper. Then they sat down to lunch on the chicken, but as they all sat down around the dish the chicken turned to life and scattered the pepper in the eyes of the Jews who were immediately blinded. There were other Jews around, however, and not all were blind, so Jesus did not escape from them. As they walked along again, Jesus bearing the cross, the Jews kept whipping Jesus, and every drop of blood that he bled along the road became an ocotee tree [a variety of resinous tree]. There were many cacti in the road, but they parted in Jesus' path.

Finally they came to the spot, and they crucified Jesus. While nailed to the cross, Jesus miraculously turned around completely, exposing his back, and from his back came maize—white, yellow, and black—and beans and potatoes and all the other food plants. Then Jesus died. Jesus was buried. But three days later, a little before 3 A.M. (when the roosters crow) Jesus was resurrected and he went to heaven. There was a large stone over his grave, and Jesus stood on it and with one foot "took off" for heaven. There remained his footprint on the stone.

Jesus stayed three days in heaven, and then he came back to earth to judge the living and the dead. The earth was overturned, and the Jews all went to Hell. On earth Jesus ordered cofradias, churches, santos, idols, rituals, and marriages, but since all the other people (the Jews) were dead and in Hell, only the Apostles were here to be ordered about. Jesus had a crown of metal thorns (espinas). There were no people on earth except the Apostles.

Jesus ordered, when we came, that there be a garden in each of the five thousand pueblos of the world. In one garden he ordered the thirteenth (and lowest) apostle to be the gardener. This gardener's name was Adam. Adam was very sad. The second apostle saw this and asked him if he was happy or sad. Adam said he was sad, because he had no company, such as a woman.

The second apostle told Jesus, and Jesus said it would be well to look for a woman for Adam. Jesus came to earth and made Adam sleep soundly. Jesus and the 12 apostles had a conference. Jesus asked the first apostle what they should do about getting a woman for Adam. The reply was that they should cut some flesh from Adam's palm. But Our Lord Jesus said this would not do because then the man would hit the woman with his hand. He asked the second apostle who advised cutting the flesh from the sole of Adam's foot to make a woman. Jesus said no, because then Adam would kick her. The third advised that they should take it from Adam's brain and head. No, replied Jesus again, for then the woman would order Adam around. The fourth apostle suggested that they cut a hole in Adam's left chest and take pieces of the heart, lungs, spleen, and other organs together with the flesh cut out, to make the woman. It should all be cut out of the left side, because if it were from the right side the woman would be higher and could command the man; the piece of heart should be taken so that the man would have a "good heart" for the woman (i.e., love her and not fight with her). To this all agreed, and Jesus blessed the pieces which had been cut from Adam and laid to his left, and immediately there was a woman.

Jesus told Adam to wake up, and Adam did so, and rose—not knowing from whence came the woman. But he took the woman with him. Jesus told Adam that when in the garden roads, the woman should always walk first. (Today all Indians have their women walking ahead of them.)

In a short time (perhaps three months) the couple saw a snake in the garden *mazacuata* (a species of constrictor). Adam and his wife did not know what life was; nor did they have clothes.

The snake caused the woman to become pregnant. This was the first time. Later came children and midwives. When the first child was born, Jesus told them they should baptize it and all future children in the church because the snake had made the woman pregnant, and it was an animal, and this was bad unless the children were baptized and made Christians. Only when baptized would the children be people (i.e., Christians).

Source: Adapted from "Jesus," Sol Tax, "Folk Tales in Chichicastenango: An Unsolved Puzzle." *Journal of American Folklore* 62 (1949): 125–135, pp. 125–128.

The Peak of Gold

Fables of golden cities and inexhaustible wealth provided powerful motivation for the early Spanish explorers of the New World. Treasure tales have found a secure home in the Latino repertoire of the Southwest over the past five centuries. "The Peak of Gold" attempts to flesh out the legend of Bernardo De Castro, a lesser-known treasure hunter who followed, literally, in the footsteps of the Conquistadors. The collector and editor of De Castro's saga, Charles F. Lummis, deserves a brief note here as well. Lummis was an author, publisher, social activist, and amateur folklorist whose work in the late nineteenth and early twentieth centuries sought to advance the cause of both Native American and Latino traditional cultures of the Southwest in an era when these cultures were in a socially and politically precarious situation. Other tales from Lummis in the present volume are "A New Mexico David," "Pablo Apodaca and the Bear," "The Penitent Brothers," "Three Live Witches," and "The Witch Deer."

The most remarkable myths that appear in American history are those which were so eagerly listened to by the early Spanish conquerors, who overran two-thirds of the two Americas long before the Saxons so much as attempted a foothold in the New World. There was the famous myth of El Dorado in South America a living man covered from head to foot with pure gold dust and nuggets. In Mexico was the fable of Montezuma's untold tons of gold and bushels of precious stones, and many other impossible things. Ponce de Leon, the gallant conqueror of Puerto Rico, paid with his life for the credulity which led him to the first of our states ever entered by a European, in quest of an alleged fountain of perpetual youth—a butterfly which some of the world's learned doctors are still chasing under another form. And all across the arid Southwest the hot winds have scattered the dust of brave but too-believing men who fell in the desert through which they pursued some glittering shape of the American golden fleece.

When Alvar Nunez Cabeza de Vaca, the first American traveler, walked across this continent from ocean to ocean, over three hundred and fifty years ago, he heard from the Indians many gilded myths, and chief of them were those concerning the famous Seven Cities of Cibola. So enormously abundant was gold said to be in these Indian cities, that it was put to the meanest uses.

When Vaca got to the Spanish settlements in Mexico and told this wonderful report it made a great commotion, and soon afterward that great explorer, Francisco Vasquez de Coronado, came to the Seven Cities of Cibola which surrounded the site of the present Pueblo Indian town of Zuni in the extreme west of New Mexico. But instead of the dazzling cities he expected, Coronado found only seven adobe towns, without an ounce of gold (or any other metal, for that matter) towns which were wonderfully curious, but which sorely disheartened the brave Spanish pioneers.

A little later Coronado heard equally astounding tales of a still more golden aboriginal city the fabulous Gran Quivira and set out to find it. After a marvelous march which took him almost to where Kansas City now is, he found the Quivira but no gold, of course. And it has been the same ever since. Coronado's footsore men ran down their fables in 1541.

Certainly not a decade, and very likely not a year, has passed since then in which some equally preposterous story of incalculable treasures has not been born and found followers in the Southwest. I know of but one thing in the world more remarkable than that the Spaniards should have believed such self-evident myths; and that one thing is that so many, many Americans believe them today.

Not long ago I visited the most remote and inaccessible ruins in the Southwest, and found there the work of these sanguine dupes, who had actually dug through solid rock in search of buried treasure. And even while I write a party is digging, a hundred miles to the west, for a treasure as mythical, and as palpably so, as that at the end of the rainbow. The stories of golden mountains, of buried millions and of mysterious "lost mines" far richer, of course, than those which any one can find in New Mexico alone would fill a volume.

I had once the good fortune to run across some old and fragmentary Spanish manuscripts of the last century and the beginning of this, which are extremely interesting. It is not often that we get so much documentary evidence concerning the golden will-o-the-wisps which have lured so many to disappointment and death. The writings all bear the stamp of implicit belief, and the old soldier, in particular, who is the hero of the fragmentary story, is often unconsciously eloquent and sometimes pathetic in his recital. I translate all the documents literally.

The first manuscript is a certified copy (certified in the City of Mexico, March 5, 1803), of the "relation" and petition of Bernardo de Castro, a copy for which the Spanish governor of New Mexico had sent. Bernardo's story and appeal are as follows, rendering as closely as possible the quaint language of the day:

> Most Excellent Sir: Bernardo de Castro, retired sergeant of the company of San Carlos [St. Charles] of the government of the City of Chihuahua, in the

Provinces of the Interior, admitted to citizenship in the City of Santa Fe, capital of the kingdom of New Mexico, and resident of this capital, goes on and before Your Excellency says: That having served our Royal Monarch for the space of nine years and eight months as sergeant of the said company in the countless combats at which I assisted against the nations of the infidels [Indians], I came out with a lance-thrust in one leg, of the which it resulted that I was placed in the invalid corps by the Sir Commander Don Juan de Ugalde. But considering that with time and medicines I recovered and gained strength to seek my subsistence free from the hardships to which the frontier troop is exposed from the Mecos [probably the Apaches], I gave up for the benefit of the royal exchequer my pay as invalid sergeant, and have followed working in the same kingdom of New Mexico. There I have suffered various fights as it befell in the past year of 1798, that while I was conducting a multitude of large cattle and other effects, the whole valued at more than $14,000, from New Mexico to El Paso del Norte [modern El Paso, Texas], the barbarous Mecos assailed me, and after a long battle, in which flowed much human blood, they carried off all I had in the world. And we gave to God thanks for having saved us even the life.

This continual contact with the savages has contracted me a friendship with the Comanche nation, which is at peace with the Spaniards, and understanding their idiom facilitates me in trading with them to gain my livelihood.

In the past year, 1798, I arrived in Santa Fe and presented myself to the Sir Governor Don Fernando Chacon. His Lordship informed me that there had come a Frenchman and had shown him a piece of metal of fine gold, assuring him he knew the spot where it was produced, and that it was a peak which the infidel nations called Peak of the Gold, where there was such an abundant breeding-place of this precious metal that all the peak and even its surroundings could with propriety be said to be pure gold. That he offered to show the spot if his Lordship would guard him with three hundred men of troops, and this he was bound to grant for the benefit of our monarch. That the distance, he considered, would be a matter of eight or nine days journey. The faithful love to our Sovereign animated the Sir Governor, and he supplied the escort which had marched two days before, and his said Lordship informed me that if he had found me in the city he would have made me one of the commanders. This offer inspired me, and I offered to follow after the expedition, and the love with which I have always served my lord, the King, enabled me by the utmost exertion to overtake the expedition, with which I incorporated myself on the third day.

And journeying on our course, on the ninth day the French guide slipped away from us, leaving us in the plains without knowledge of the road to our desired peak. At the which it was resolved by the leaders of the expedition to return to Santa Fe. But I, not suffering from the short march, separated from the expedition and went on alone to verify the report. And in the rancherias [villages] of the Comanches, where I was entertained, when I told them the trick and the mockery that the Frenchman had put upon us, they assured me with one accord that the said Frenchman did not know the location of the peak at all, and that he had never been there, for the gold which he took to New Mexico they themselves had given him in exchange for various trinkets of coral, belts and other trifles. But that they knew the peak of gold, that was indeed with an abundance never seen before, and if I would go with them they would show me it, and I could pick up all I wished, and if we met any other nation [of Indians] I should not be harmed if with them, for they were all friends.

Indeed, most illustrious Sir, only by my fidelity and obedience to my superior could I contain myself not to march to the peak without delay; and I told my friends the Mecos Comanches, that I was going to seek permission of that Sir Governor of the New Mexico, and with it would return. I arrived in Santa Fe and sought that permission, but it was denied me. But continuing my visits to the Mequeria [I find that] so strong a desire have they formed for the granting of that permission and the development of this treasure, and the facility there is that the Spaniards enjoy it and that their Sovereign make heavy his royal coffers, that I resolved to make a walk of more than seven hundred leagues to seek the aid and encouragement of Your excellency.

The brave sergeant so fully believed in his Peak of Gold that he actually walked nearly 2,200 miles alone through a most dangerous country to lay the matter before the Viceroy in Mexico.

My plan being approved, it is undeniable that the Royal treasury will be swelled by the tithes and dues to the Royal crown; new interest will animate men to follow up the discovery, and there will be civilized (with time and the friendship which is contracted with the nations of the Comanches, Yutas [Utes] and Navajosos [Navajos]) more than three hundred leagues of virgin and powerful lands that being reckoned the distance from the city of Santa Fe to the Peak of Gold. The inhabitants of the internal provinces, who now live under the yoke of the assaults of the hostile Indians, will revive; it will be easier for the Sovereign to guard the frontiers of these his vast dominions. Settlements will be made, and insensibly will follow the conquest and pacification of the infidels, who will easily embrace the holy Gospel and come under the faith of Jesus Christ. What results to religion, to the monarch and to his vassals are presented, even by this clumsy narration!

I do not intend to burden the Royal treasury with the slightest expense, nor do I think to involve the Royal arms in actions which might imperil the troops. My person is declared past its usefulness for the Royal service, and I count myself as a dead man for entering matters of importance. But my military spirit does not falter, and I only desire to manifest, even at the foot of the tomb, my love to my Sovereign. With only one faithful companion I intend to go among my friends, the Comanches, and, with the protection and guidance of them, to enter and explore the land, silently, without noise or preparation, to force a passage.

Quietness, the gray shadows of the night and our own courage are the only preparations I make for the difficult undertaking, and, above all, the divine aid. Having found the desired Peak of Gold, charted the roads to it, made the due surveys, and gathered so much of the precious metal as we can transport without making danger (and under the divine favor), I will present myself again to Your Excellency, and by your Superiority will be taken such steps as the state of the case demands.

Under which considerations, and the solid arguments which I have expressed, of which Your Excellency can receive full confirmation from the most excellent Senor Don Pedro de Nava, commander-in-chief of the interior provinces, and Don Joseph Casiano Feaomil y Garay, lieutenant-captain of dragoons of San Luis Potosi, I humbly beg of Your Excellency that in use of your Viceroyal powers, you deign to grant me your superior permission to go in search of the Peak of Gold; being kind enough to send to the Senor Don Fernando Chacon, actual Governor of the New Mexico, that he put no difficulty in my path, and giving orders to the captains and chiefs of the friendly nations Comanches, Yutas and Navajosos that they accompany and guide me in this expedition.

And I respectfully say that my delay in getting to this Capital [the City of Mexico] was because I had to come nearly all the way on foot, my horse having given out in that great distance, and that now I am supported here by alms, such is my great anxiety for the benefit of the monarch, and beg that I be excused for this paper. [He was too poor to buy the stamped and taxed paper on which petitions to the Viceroy must be addressed.]

For so much I pray Your Excellency's favor. BERNARDO CASTRO.

He had the real spirit of the Argonauts, this crippled old soldier, to whom poverty and danger and 2,000 mile walks were trifles when they stood between him and his Peak of Gold.

The Viceroy evidently gave the desired permission without which, under the strict Spanish laws, no such venture was to be thought of and there were one or more expeditions, but unfortunately we have left no account of them. It is clear that the Viceroy ordered Governor Chacon, of New Mexico, to assist Castro in his undertaking, and that the matter aroused a good deal of interest throughout the provinces of New Spain. Don Nemecio Salcedo, military commandant at Chihuahua, seems to have interested himself in the matter, for the next document in this fragmentary series is a draft of a reply to him from Governor Chacon, as follows.

According to that which Your Lordship advises me in communication of the 16th of September of the current year, I repeat that as to the expedition of Bernardo Castro to the discovery of the Peak of Gold, I will help him and the others who accompany him, that they may have no difficulty with the General of the Comanches, whom, however, I have not yet seen, since he has not yet returned with the ransom he offered me when he was last in this capital.

There was other correspondence between these two on the same matter, for now we come to an original letter from Commandant Salcedo to Governor Chacon, replying to a late one of his. It says:

The communication of Your Lordship, of the 18th of last November, leaves me informed of all the assistances you gave Bernardo Castro, that he might undertake the second journey [so he had already made one] from that city, with the object to discover the Peak of Gold, which he has described in the territory of that province. And of the results I hope Your Lordship will give me account.

Poor brave, misguided Bernardo de Castro! I wish we might have more of the documents about his venturesome wanderings in quest of the Peak of Gold. He must have gone far out into the wastes of Texas; and at last he, too, yielded up his life, as did countless of his countrymen before him, to that deadliest of yellow fevers. We lose all track of him until Governor Chaves writes from Santa Fe, in 1829, to his superior in the City of Mexico, who had written to ask him about these and other matters. His letter says:

Most Excellent Sir: In compliance with that which Your Excellency requests in your official letter of the 19th of August last, that I make the necessary verifications upon the mineral reported by the Rev. Father Custodian of these missions, Fray Sevastian Alvares, to be found among the gentile Comanches, I have investigated the matter, and place in the knowledge of Your Excellency that which various of the citizens of this capital and all of them most veracious say. They all agree in that it is a fact that Don Bernardo de Castro [the old soldier had evidently won honorable recognition, else a Governor of New Mexico would not speak of him by the respectful title of "Don"] entered this territory with the object of seeking the said mineral; that he made various expeditions with this object, until in one of them he was slain by the heathen Apaches.

Passing to information received from the travelers to that nation, all agree in the statement that the Comanches offer to sell them pouches filled with a metal which appears fine and of great weight, which they say they get from the neighborhood of the Ash peaks (which are very well known to our people, but not explored or charted, because they are distant from the trails).

The citizen Pablo Martin has been he who expressed himself most fully. He, knowing that the said Don Bernardo de Castro sought a mineral in the Comanche nation, has procured them to look for the said mineral. The only result was that one Comanche named *Pano de Lienso* [Cloth of Linen], who made himself his companion, gave him information that beyond the Ash peaks, in some round hills, were stones with much silver, whereof the said Comanche had carried some to the province of San Antonio de Bejar [Texas], where they made buttons for him. He who made the buttons charged the Comanche to bring him a load [of that metal], but he did not do so, because in that time came the war of his people with that province. Other Comanches also have told him [Pablo Martin] that in said spot were stones with silver.

This is all I have been able to find out as the results of my investigations, the which I place in the knowledge of Your Excellency, that you may put it to the use which you deem best.

SANTA FEE, 30 of October of 1829.

CHAVES.

And there, so far as we know it now, is the story of the Peak of Gold.

Source: Adapted from "The Peak of Gold," Charles F. Lummis. *The Enchanted Burro and Other Stories as I Have Known Them from Maine to Chile and California* (Chicago: A. C. McClurg & Co., 1912), pp. 162–174.

Becoming American

The following oral biography relates the childhood experiences of Guadalupe ("Lupita") Gallegos, an affluent Latino woman living in New Mexico between its annexation following the Mexican-American War (1846–1848) and prior to its becoming a state in 1912. The narrative provides insights into race relations, family life, and the impact of political conflict on daily affairs.

In the face of Guadalupe, "Lupita," Gallegos is written the story of a long and interesting life—a life that has had more than its share of heartaches and happiness. It is a kind, intelligent face and devout.

She dresses in unrelieved black. On her head is worn a tight-fitting cap with ribbons tied under her chin in a bow. Around her slender shoulders is wrapped a black Spanish shawl. Her blouse and skirt are black and on her feet she wears tiny, patent-leather shoes.

When asked a question about some incident of long ago there flashes in her eyes the look of a girl, she smiles half-wistfully, and begins:

I was born in Las Vegas, New Mexico on December 12, 1855. I was baptized by Father Pinal, a French Priest.

My parents, Severo Baca and Maria Ignacia, were wealthy, owning several farms, many cattle and sheep, and much money and jewelry. My great grandfather, Santiago Ulibarri, had several children, but I was his only great granddaughter and so I was his pet. Mr. Ulibarri was tall, blond, and green-eyed, and very wealthy.

His home was Spanish with all the windows opening on the *placita*, a large yard in the middle. This house was very dark and gloomy and was open to no one except a few Spanish friends. When one entered one of those old Spanish houses it seemed as if one were entering a tomb, so cold and uninviting were they. Several families would live in these houses; the owner's children, their husbands and wives, and their children.

We lived there shut away from the rest of the world. Mr. Ulibarri was the head of his household and he knew it. He was virtually the dictator of his family. The women were never allowed on the streets without someone trustworthy to escort them. We obeyed Mr. Ulibarri in everything. Only that which he dictated was done.

Since it was considered such a disgrace for a lady of the upper class to be seen on the street unescorted, we spent most of our time sewing, and playing the piano. We never dreamed of soiling our hands in the kitchen cooking or cleaning.

In front of Mr. Ulibarri we were always very dignified and well-behaved, but when he was not present we were often silly, as most girls are. I was the only one of the girls who was permitted to go with Mr. Ulibarri very often. He would have his chocolate in bed about eleven o'clock, arise later and have his regular breakfast. Then he would say to the servants in a commanding voice, "Lousiana, my cape, my cane, and my hat."

The servants would rush to do his bidding. Then he would say, "Lupita, come to me."

"Oh! no! no!" protested the servants, "She is all dirty. Let us wash her."

"You wash yourself. Leave her alone," Mr. Ulibarri would say in a very patient voice.

Then he would go to different stores with little Lupita holding his hand. Immediately upon entering a store, Lupita would go to the candy counter and help herself.

One day when Mr. Ulibarri was away all the woman got together. They had heard of a strange new toy that had just come to Andres Dol's store. They were very anxious to see it, so much so, indeed, that they sneaked out of the house and went to town to see it. The new toy was a jack-in-the-box. The women had a good time at the store and when they returned home they made Lupita promise not to tell on them.

Later in the afternoon Mr. Ulibarri returned home looking very pleased. He called all of his children, servants, and relatives together and told them he had a surprise for them. He laid a large box on the table and told one of the girls to open it. When she opened the box out jumped the jack-in-the-box. Of course everyone was surprised. Only Lupita was unimpressed, "Oh! I have seen it already!" she blurted out.

"What, my child?" asked her great grandfather. Before she had a chance to answer Lupita was carried away to another room and scolded.

Lupita had a Negro nurse who was called Lorenza. She had been brought to Las Vegas by Mr. Ulibarri who had bought her from the Comanche Indians when she was only seven years old. It is believed that she was the first Negress brought into Las Vegas. People from far and near came to see her. Lupita says it was very pleasant to kiss Lorenza because of her soft, thick lips.

Governor Manual Armijo was Maria Ignacia's [Lupita's mother] father's first cousin. He sent word one day from Tecolote that he was coming to Las Vegas to visit his cousin and that he wanted the family to have some delicious hot tamales ready when he arrived.

The Governor was in Tecolote already! The house was in an uproar. Servants set to work cleaning the house and cooking chili.

Maria Ignacia was in the kitchen when Governor Armijo arrived. She had never seen a governor before, and she was anxious to see what one looked like. She took a bag of tobacco and ran into the room. "Mother, here's your tobacco!"

Her mother was embarrassed, "Go and wash yourself," she said.

"Oh, no!" said Governor Armijo, "don't send her away. Come to me, my child."

Maria Ignacia ran to him and jumped upon his lap, spilling the cup of chocolate which he held in his hand all over his trousers, Maria Ignacia's mother was very embarrassed, but the Governor only laughed.

When Lupita was eight years old Santiage Ulibarri died and left her an inheritance.

When the Civil War broke out Lupita was sick with fever and her father wanted to take her south, but her mother refused, because the sympathies of the New Mexicans were with the North.

In her home Lupita was a regular princess. She was the only child and had everything she desired. At noon the servants would come to dress her. Then she would come downstairs, roam through the yard, or play with her toys, or go visiting with her parents.

She had an old tutor who taught her to read, write, and to work out problems in arithmetic. When she was ten years old she attended the Loretto Academy in Santa Fe. She had been there only seven months when a fever epidemic broke out, and her parents sent for her at once. She was taught to embroider, to play the piano, and only such things that would make a lady of her.

Lupita's mother, Maria Ignacia, was just a little girl when General Kearny came to Las Vegas to take possession of the territory. Maria Ignacia's father got up unusually early and went for a walk. Where the Normal University now stands he saw a many cannons all pointing toward the town. Immediately he rushed to town to spread the news. The town was in an uproar. Everyone, it seemed was screaming and crying. None wanted to become Americans; all wanted to remain under the Mexican flag.

Maria Ignacia's father refused at first to become an American. He left everything he owned and went to Mexico. All his land confiscated, his stock was killed to feed the troops, and only his house remained to him.

The family which Mr. Ulibarri had been the head of for so many happy years moved to San Miguel. After a year Hillario Gonzales, head of the family, came back to Las Vegas. He made friends with Kearny, regained some of his possessions and moved into his house where some of the troops had been lodged. Gonzales sent to San Miguel for his family and when they arrived General Kearny, his wife and their six year old daughter moved in with them. The little girl was pretty, having fair hair and blue eyes. General Kearny's men were fed on the cows, sheep, and other stock belonging to Hillario Gonzales.

Source: The Biography of Guadalupe, "Lupita," Gallegos. Lynn Bright. American Life Histories: Manuscripts from the Federal Writers' Project, 1936–1940. Ms. Div., Lib. of Congress. *American Memory.* Lib. of Congress, Washington. August 7, 2008. http://memory.loc.gov/ammem/wpaintro/wpahome.html.

HEROES, HEROINES, VILLAINS, AND FOOLS

The Little Green Rabbit

The following tale is heavily influenced by the European Märchen (in English this tale genre is usually labeled "fairy tale" or "wonder tale"). This influence is seen in the relatively complex plot, patterns of threes (for example, three brothers), and long-suffering central characters pitted against a cruel parental authority. Unlike many of the traditional European tales popularized in contemporary films, a female protagonist is cast as the heroic figure who must take on a quest in order to rescue her victimized suitor.

Long ago there was a very rich king who had three sons—three very handsome sons whom he loved very much. The king, however, desired to have his orders obeyed implicitly. One day the three princes went visiting without their father's permission, and the king became so angry that he punished them by enchanting them and transforming them into little rabbits. The eldest was changed into a pinto rabbit, the second into a white rabbit, and the youngest into a very pretty little green rabbit.

Furthermore, the king told them, "For an entire year you will not leave the palace and will only assume your human form at night."

Time passed. One day when the three rabbits were nibbling grass in the palace garden, the green rabbit said, "Hermanos [brothers], I can't bear this life any longer. Let us crawl through the water pipe and see what surrounds this prison."

The other two rabbits were loath to go. They were afraid of the king. However, the green rabbit insisted so much that finally the brothers agreed. All that afternoon the rabbits ran over the hill and dale. Returning to the palace, they heard the beautiful voice of someone singing a happy song.

"Let us go and see who is singing," said the green rabbit.

His brothers refused, even though the green rabbit begged and begged. The green rabbit went alone. He went in the direction the singing came from and found a beautiful palace. Hoping to find a way to get in, he hopped around the garden walls and finally found a crack through which he crawled. Silently he crept into the garden. There he saw that the singer was a beautiful princess with sun-gold hair and sea-blue eyes. Her name was Marisol. The little rabbit fell in love with her at first sight. Unconsciously, he got nearer and nearer to her. The princess, seeing the rabbit, with a single motion captured him. She ran into the palace to show her parents the pretty little green rabbit she had captured. Her parents loved Marisol very much. Besides being good and kind, Marisol was their only daughter. The princess then took the rabbit to her bedroom, and imagine her surprise when she heard the rabbit speak!

"Beautiful princess, I am not a rabbit. I am a prince enchanted as punishment for disobeying my father. If you do not let me go, my father the king will kill me tonight. Release me and I promise that as soon as my penalty is over, I will return and marry you. In token of my word, take this ring."

The princess was astonished to hear the rabbit's words, but because she was kind and because she had fallen in love with the rabbit, she took him to the garden and let him go.

Months passed and the rabbit didn't come back to see Marisol! More time went by and Marisol began to pine. To such an extent did her heartbreak increase that her parents became alarmed. They decided that in order to cheer her, a great fiesta would be given in her honor. They ordered musicians and artists to be brought from all over. Perhaps they would cheer her.

In a nearby village there lived an old man who had a daughter. The girl could play the guitar and sing gay and beautiful songs. When he heard the king's proclamation, the old man decided to take Rosita, his daughter, to sing before the princess. The girl and her father, astride their little donkey, set out for the palace. They had to pass through the city where the rabbits lived.

When they arrived there, Rosita and her father were very hungry. She went to a bakery near to the palace to buy some bread. The baker was very angry because his bread had burnt, so he hurled the flat loaf of bread at Rosita. She tried to catch it but could not. The round, flat loaf fell to the floor and rolled out of the door. Rosita ran after it, but the bread kept on rolling and rolling.

Finally, it rolled through a crack in the palace wall and lodged near the door of a beautiful bedroom in which there were three beautiful beds. Rosita heard a noise and perforce had to hide. She took cover behind the arras in the room, and peeping around it saw three rabbits come in. One was a pinto rabbit, the other a white rabbit and the third a green rabbit. The pinto rabbit jumped on the bed, flipped himself over, and became a handsome prince. The white one did the same and changed into another very handsome prince. Soon, both went to sleep. Finally, the green rabbit jumped on the bed, flipped over, and was changed into a very, very handsome prince. But this last prince did not go to sleep right away; he began to cry.

The other two princes awoke and began to talk to him saying, "Forget the Princess Marisol. Our father will never let you marry her."

At last all three princes went to sleep and Rosita managed to make her way out of the palace by the same route she had used in entering.

Dawn was near, so Rosita and her father left for Marisol's village.

Rosita and her father arrived at the palace and went to see the king. Rosita sang and danced but could make no impression on Marisol. At length, Rosita said, "Look Princess, I am going to tell you a tale."

Then Rosita related all that had happened and how she had seen the little green rabbit. Marisol was filled with joy and asked her parents for permission to go and see the green rabbit. Marisol's parents did not want to let her go, but she insisted so much that the king and queen finally agreed.

Rosita and Marisol journeyed to the city where the rabbit lived. When they were near the crack in the wall of the palace, Rosita told Marisol, "Look, my princess, we are going into the palace through this crack in the wall. Do not make any noise, for if the king hears us he will kill us."

Marisol agreed and they entered the prince's bedroom. After some time the pinto rabbit came in, jumped on the bed, flipped over and became a handsome prince. Then a white rabbit came in, did the same, and became another handsome prince. At last the little green rabbit came in, and when he had jumped on the bed and flopped over, Marisol could not stand it any longer. She cried and ran towards the prince.

The king, who had been strolling near the hall, heard Marisol cry and immediately rushed to the bedroom. When the king saw her, he was greatly angered, so much that he wanted to kill her. But then the youngest prince told his father, "My liege and my King, this maiden is my fiancée and we are going to be married."

The king's rage knew no bounds but, controlling himself he said, "So you want to get married, eh? And so you have seen each other without my consent, eh? Well, now, before I agree to your wedding you two must do as I say."

"You," he told the prince, "will continue to be a rabbit for seven more years. And you," the king told Marisol, "will not be able to marry the prince until you fill seven barrels with your tears and wear out these seven pairs of iron shoes."

The poor prince and the poor princess had to say yes. They could not do anything else. The prince knelt down and prayed and Marisol tearfully bade him good-bye as she went out into the world to wear out her iron shoes.

After walking and crying a long, long time, Marisol finally arrived at the house where the moon lived. Marisol had already filled the barrels with her tears and worn out the seven pairs of iron shoes. However, the poor girl was so tired and so far from the green rabbit's palace that she had to rest some place. Marisol knocked on the door of the moon's house, and the moon came out.

"Niña," said the moon, "what are you doing here?"

Marisol told the moon her story and asked aid in reaching the green rabbit's home.

"Look," said the moon, "at present I cannot travel through that particular part of the world. I am not due on that side of the earth for many more days. But do you see that hill? My compadre, the Sun, lives over there. Go to him, he probably will be able to help you."

Marisol walked and walked and finally arrived at the sun's house. She knocked on the door and the sun came out. "What are you doing around here, niña?" asked the sun.

"I am the green rabbit's fiancée," said Marisol. "I am wondering if you could aid me in getting back to his palace."

The sun stared at Marisol and said, "Do you say you are the green rabbit's fiancée? That is impossible. The green rabbit is going to be married within three days. His fiancée was picked out by the king himself. All the people are praying for me to be in a good humor. They really want me to shine that day."

"Señor Sol," begged Marisol, "please take me to the palace." And the girl told the sun all that had happened to her.

"Look, niña," answered the sun, "I cannot take you because if I held you in my arms I would burn you. But listen! Yonder, on the other side of that hill, lives my compadre, the Wind. Tell him to take you where you are going."

Marisol walked and walked until finally reaching the hill, went to the house where the wind lived. The girl knocked on the door and Señora Aire, the wind's wife, came out.

"Come in, hijita [little daughter]," Señora Aire said, "what are you doing around here?"

Marisol told Señora Aire all that had happened. Suddenly the Señor Aire came in, laughing so hard that he shook all over. Señora Aire asked him the reason for his laughter and Señor Aire answered that it was because he had destroyed all the preparations for the wedding of the green rabbit and his fiancée. The wind saw Marisol then, and asked her what she was doing there. Marisol told him what had befallen her.

"Oh," said Señor Aire, "that's probably the reason the green rabbit has been praying so much in the chapel lately. I think he is asking for your return. Take hold of my waist and quicker than you can wink your eye we will be at the palace."

And with whirlwind speed Señor Aire took Marisol to the palace where the green rabbit lived.

The king was there also and he asked, "Who is this beggar?"

But the green rabbit recognized Marisol and ran to her, crying at the same time, "My fiancée is here! My true fiancée has come at last!"

Marisol then produced the seven barrels filled with her tears and a handkerchief where the remains of the seven pairs of iron shoes were tied. She gave them to the king.

And since the king had given his word, Marisol and the prince were married and lived happily ever after.

Source: "El Conejito Verde," Gabriel A. Cordova Jr. *Magic Tales of Mexico.* M.A. Thesis. Texas Western College, El Paso, TX, 1951.http://www.genecowan.com/ magictales/, retrieved August 6, 2008.

A New Mexico David

The local legend of folk hero Lucario Montoya, although reworked into a more literary version by folklorist Charles F. Lummis, retains the marks of oral tradition. The description of the Ute chief and his horse, for example, seem highly exaggerated and included during the process of oral transmission in order to amplify the prowess of young Lucario. The narrative also enhances the modern reader's understanding of relationships between New Mexicans of Spanish descent and specific groups of Native Americans with who Hispanic settlers shared the territory.

I doubt very much if Lucario Montoya had ever heard of that wonderful fight of long ago between the shepherd stripling and Goliath of Gath. Certainly he had never read of those things, for a book would have been the most incomprehensible of mysteries to Lucario. But in the great and wonderful volume of "Out-of-Doors" he was an apt scholar in that he had had the most learned of schoolmasters—his Mexican father and his Indian acquaintances.

He could go out into the traveled road and read from the strangling hieroglyphics of the dust how long it had been since the last party passed; whether they were Mexicans or Indians, men or women, traveling ... fast or slowly, by night or by day. He could not read it half so well as an Indian, but he was a famous trailer none the less.

In all outdoor sports, too, that were known then and there, he was an expert. When, on their feast days, the young men of Cebolleta used to bury a rooster to its wattles in the sand, and mounting their horses two hundred yards away ride down in a whirlwind gallop, swinging low from the saddle to pluck up that tiny mark as they thundered past, it was Lucario oftener than any other who swept triumphant down the valley with half a hundred reckless riders in mad pursuit; with shrill yells swinging that feathered club about his head to fight off those who grappled him. Pistols there were none in New Mexico in those days, and of guns only the old Spanish flintlock muskets. But with bow and arrows Lucario won many a pony and gay blanket in matches with the Navajos and Utes. With the *reata* [lariat] he was equally skilful, and more than once had lassoed antelope in the prairies a feat of which the most practiced "roper" might well feel proud.

Above all, he could throw the knife. It was the favorite weapon of his race, and one in the deadly use of which they have never been excelled. Many an Indian had bitten the dust in the hand-to-hand struggles which were then so common between the settlers and their savage neighbors pierced through and through by the shining *cuchillo largo* [long knife] of some brave Cebolletan. Ever since his boyhood Lucario had practiced throwing his knife, and now from four feet away he could drive it, quivering, two inches deep into a foot circle of wood. With the arm hanging at full length, he placed the knife point forward in the open palm. Then he shoved his arm suddenly forward, with a sort of scooping motion, and off flew the glittering missile.

All this Lucrio was at home in; but if you had shown him a book, with those funny little black things chasing each other across the white paper, I am sorry to say he would have been quite lost.

Lucario was a shepherd, and tended one of the flocks of Don Refugio when the Indians were sufficiently quiet to permit any sallying forth from the little walled town. Though known for his athletic accomplishments, he was neither tall nor very muscular, but an ordinary lad of seventeen, who might weigh one hundred and twenty pounds, but making up in wiriness, skill, and agility what he lacked in brute strength. His straight, jet hair fell below his shoulders; his face just showing a faint, dark fuzz was thin, but with a vivid red shining through the olive skin, and his black eyes were large and wonderfully bright.

It was in 1840 eight years before New Mexico became part of the United States. It was then the Province of New Mexico a colony of Old Mexico, and governed by a Viceroy sent thence.

Of our race, who arrogate to themselves distinctively the name "Americans," there were hardly any in the province—perhaps a dozen in all. But of the descendants of the hardy Spanish pioneers who became Americans long before any English-speaking people did, there were many thousands. But they were heavily outnumbered by the Indians, of whom there were many powerful, hostile tribes. The Pueblos, a race of quiet farmers who dwelt in as good houses as the Mexicans themselves, had made their last protest, more than a century before, against the occupancy of the Spanish, and were now excellent neighbors. But the Apaches, the Nayajos, the Utes, the Piutes, the Uncompahgres, and the Comanches had never been conquered, and were incessantly warring upon the settlers. Lucario's father, mother, grandfather, great-grandfather, five uncles, two older brothers, and I know not how many more distant relatives, had all been killed by the Indians, and his was by no means an unparalleled case of bereavement.

This year the Utes had been doing their cruelest work in Western New Mexico. They had surprised several hamlets and massacred all in them, had cut off many shepherds, stolen many thousand sheep, and made unsuccessful but disastrous assaults upon Cebolleta and other small fortified towns. It had become unbearable, and the chief men throughout New Mexico had met and subscribed money to send out against the Indians a thousand volunteers under the command of the brave Manuel Chaves. Lucario's only surviving uncle—his father's eldest brother—was second in command; and Lucario's great delight, was allowed to join the expedition.

The force marched far northward, past the Cabezon ("Big Head") a strange peak of rock apparently larger at the top than at the bottom. Two days later, they camped in the plains below the giant range of Jemez, having sighted a large force of Utes in the timber ahead. The New Mexicans, who were outnumbered four to one, entrenched themselves as best they might, to await the attack. The Utes came skimming about the camp on their fleet horses, with taunting gestures, but taking good care to keep beyond the range of the flintlocks.

One gigantic savage, mounted upon a large and snow white mustang, made himself particularly conspicuous. He was plainly a chief. His buckskin suit of soft black was beautifully fringed, and resplendent with silver buttons. He was fully seven feet tall, and immensely broad across the shoulders. His horsemanship was wonderful, and the brave New Mexicans, who could appreciate the good points of even an enemy, were lost in admiration.

"Ah! Que guapo" ["How handsome"], they cried as he swept past them like the wind, now vaulting to his feet in the saddle, now altogether disappearing on the farther side of his horse, and shooting arrows at them from under the horse's neck with astonishing force and accuracy, and now leaping from saddle to ground and back from ground to saddle, all without a break in his mad gallop.

"Who dares come out into the plain and fight me alone?" he cried, suddenly wheeling his horse and riding broadside past them, not more than a hundred yards away. "If you have any great warrior, let him come. If I kill him, you shall go back to your homes and follow us no more. But if he kills me, then my people will return to the country of the Utes, and end the war."

There were brave men in plenty among the New Mexicans, and I doubt not that many volunteers might have been found to take up the huge Ute's challenge. But before any one else had stirred, Lucario ran to his uncle, who was talking with Colonel Chaves.

"Uncle," he said, "I am young, and the last of the family. Let me go out to this boastful barbarian! If I die, there are none to mourn; but if I kill him, with the help of San Esteban, then we are relieved from war, and you shall feel proud of your brother's son."

Don Jose was a man of rough exterior, though of a good heart. Brave himself, he admired bravery and loathed cowardice. "Go, then," he said gruffly, "but look that thou kill him! Come back without his head, and I will kill thee!"

"And if thou bring his head," said Colonel Chaves, "I will make thee a captain this very day!"

Lucario waited to hear no more. Running to where his pet pony Alazan was picketed, he pulled up the picket-pin and removed it from his long *reata* of braided horsehair. Having taken all the kinks out of the rope and seen that the noose would run easily through its loop, he coiled and hung it upon his saddle-bow. He loosened the heavy knife in its sheath, which was sewed upon the side of his buckskin breeches, tested the arrows in his quiver to be sure that they were all well feathered; and leaping lightly to the saddle, rode slowly out into the plain with a quiet, "Good-bye, my friends."

When the Utes saw how small was the horse, and what a slender stripling its rider, they set up yells of derisive laughter. The giant chief was particularly merry, and rode down toward Lucario slowly, showing his large white teeth, and calling, "Are there no men among you, that you send out a child to me for a mouthful?"

Most of the New Mexicans were somewhat familiar with the language of the Utes, and Lucario understood the taunt perfectly. "Truly, I am but a small mouthful," he called back, "but perhaps a bitter one! We shall see."

When he was within fifty yards, he sent a sudden arrow whistling at his huge foe. The motion was so cat-like and unexpected that the Ute had scarce time to "duck" to the side of his horse, and the arrow pierced his ear.

With a grunt of mingled astonishment and appreciation of the lad's skill the Indian drew his own heavy bow, giving the string a tug that would have sent its shaft through a buffalo. But Lucario was watching, and when the arrow came, it passed a foot above the saddle, and found nothing there.

His own second arrow merely grazed the Ute's horse; and now, seeing that he had no ordinary marksman to deal with, the Indian clung to his horse's side and began galloping around and around Lucario, shooting at him from under the horse's neck, but never exposing so much of himself as a whole hand. Lucario adopted the same tactics, and so skillfully, that in a few minutes each had spent all his arrows, and neither was more than scratched.

The Utes had all ridden out from the timber, and were drawn up in an irregular line a few hundred feet away, watching the curious fight with intense interest. About as far away on the other side were the New Mexicans, who had also mounted to get a better view.

Lucario swung erect into his saddle. "With the reata!" he shouted, uncoiling his own rope, and running it rapidly through his hands till he had the long running-noose ready and trailing from his right hand back upon the ground. The Ute understood, and did likewise. Then they went galloping around each other, wheeling, charging, dodging, swinging the long nooses around their heads, and watching their chance. The horses understood this game as well as their riders, and played as important a part in it. Both were rough-haired; but their deer-like legs, small fine heads, and arching necks bespoke their descent from the noble Arab steeds brought here by the Spanish Conquistadores in 1541, the first horses in America, and ancestors of all the "wild horses" of the plains.

Lucario soon found this a very different business from lassoing even antelope. It took all his quickness of eye and all his agility to keep that deadly
noose from settling down over his own neck. At last the Indian let the reata
fly suddenly as he was passing, at the same instant wheeling his horse inward
to gain the necessary distance. He had calculated wonderfully well, and the
move was too quick for Lucario, but Alazan had seen it and made a mighty
sidewise bound. The noose swept across his flanks and fell empty to the
ground, and Lucario, as his intelligent horse wheeled back with wonderful
rapidity, dropped his own rope deftly over the head of the Indian before
the latter had recovered himself. Giving a quick turn of the rope around
his saddle-bow, the boy touched the spurs to Alazan.

For an instant it looked as though he "had" the Indian, and would unseat
and drag him to death, and the New Mexicans yelled exultantly. But the vast
strength of the Ute, and the quickness and superior weight of his horse,
saved him. Snatching the taut rope with his brawny arms, he gave it a turn
around his saddle-bow, lifted the relieved noose over his head, and cut it
with his knife.

His face was no longer smiling, but contorted with savage passions.
He forgot his challenge to a fair combat, and now thought only of killing
this saucy boy and saving himself from disgrace, if not death.

He began circling again around Lucario, all the time stealthily edging
nearer to his people. Suddenly one of them dashed out from the line and
tossed him a long, sharp lance. He caught it deftly, and brandishing it aloft
came charging down upon Lucario like a thunderbolt.

For an instant the boy was dumbfounded by this treachery. His arrows
gone, his reata useless should he fly? No! He knew well that his stern uncle
had meant every word; he would rather see him dead than in flight.
Ah! His knife! He whipped it from its sheath and held it down beside him,
putting Alazan to a gentle canter toward the Ute. They were not more than
fifteen yards apart in an instant the shock must come. And then, his big eyes
shining like coals, Lucario rose suddenly in his stirrups with a flashing, overhead motion of his right arm, and dug the rowels into Alazan's flanks, twisting his head sharply to the left.

The Ute giant swayed in his saddle and lurched heavily to the ground,
while his scared horse went on down the valley like the wind. The New
Mexicans dashed forward, and snatching the fainting Lucario from his saddle, carried him into camp. The Ute had hurled his heavy lance at the same
instant, and it had passed through Lucario's arm, making a ghastly hole.
But when they went to the fallen giant, he was quite dead. The boy's heavy
knife had smitten him squarely between the eyes; and stout Patricio had to
press his heel upon the Ute's throat before he could tug out the bedded blade.

According to the compact, the Utes were already galloping away; and it
was many months before they made another foray into that portion of
New Mexico.

Lucario recovered from his wound, and distinguished himself as a captain in several subsequent Indian wars. He bade fair to become one of the noted men of New Mexico; but in January, 1850, he was among the victims of that bloody night at San Miguel, when the lurking Apaches surprised and massacred the flower of New Mexican soldiery "the Brave Thirty of Cebolleta."

Source: "A New Mexico David," C. S. Lummis. *A New Mexico David and Other Stories and Sketches of the Southwest* (New York: Charles Scribner's Sons, 1891), pp. 1–11.

John Tiger

"John Tiger" is a variant of the European folktale often entitled "John the Bear." In this case, however, rather than being the offspring of a human mother and a bear, the hero is the son of a tigre. Although tigre is usually translated as "jaguar," in the southwestern United States and northern Mexico the puma or the jaguarondi are more typically encountered. In any case, this represents a good example of localization of a European folktale to the Hispanic Southwest. For convenience, "tigre" is translated as "tiger" in the following tale.

A man and his wife were living on their ranch at the outskirts of a village. They had several head of cattle which they milked every day. They used part of the milk for selling, and part for making cheese. The wife was pious, almost a fanatic, and went to mass every day just before her husband finished milking; then she took the milk of the first cows along for sale, and fulfilled her religious duties at the same time.

One Sunday it happened that she urged her husband to go to mass. After they had agreed upon this, he went to church, while she remained behind to milk the cows.

Unfortunately, that day one of them did not come to the corral, and, as it was getting late, the woman went out to look for her all around the corral; but instead of finding the cow of which she was in search, she met a tiger; and before she realized what was happening, the beast carried her to his cave, where he kept her locked up many years.

During this time the poor woman lived on raw meat, which the tiger obtained from the herd of her own husband. At the end of one year the woman gave birth to a boy, the son of the tiger, who grew up, strong and fierce, like his father, but who had human form. The years passed, and the boy developed extraordinary strength. Therefore he opened the stone door of the cavern, which his mother had not been able to move with all the efforts she had made. The mother, with the tenderness that belongs to all of the mothers in the world, taught him to speak, and told him her story as soon as she thought that her son understood her.

The boy asked her one day if she wished to leave her prison, and said that he could free her by killing his own father. The woman accepted the proposal of her son, although with great fear, and made up her mind to suffer the consequences in case he should not succeed. The beast had gone out to bring meat for his family. Then the boy, who was seven years old, searched for a weapon, and found near the cave a stout and heavy pole, with which he prepared himself to murder his father.

The boy kept in hiding outside of the enormous rock which served as his mother's prison when the tiger's terrific and wild howl was heard, which terrified the poor woman inside the cave as never before. The wild beast came to the door, and, when he tried to open it, the boy gave him a tremendous blow on the head, which killed him almost immediately. A second blow ended the life of the animal, who lay there, extending his teeth and his claws for a little while, as though he wanted to imbed them in the flesh of his enemy.

The boy and his mother left the dark place in which they had passed such sad days of their existence, and traveled to the ranch of the woman's husband. As might be supposed, the woman had not even a rag with which to cover herself. While they were walking through the woods, she covered herself with leaves; but when they came near the hut, she sent her son to see the master, and to ask him for a garment for his mother, who was naked. That poor man was no other than her husband, who preserved as a sacred token of remembrance the dresses of his beloved wife, whom he believed to have been dead for many years.

The woman reached the home of her husband, to whom she did not disclose herself at once. She only asked for a room in which she and her son might sleep several days. But while these days were passing, he became convinced that she was his wife, He questioned her one day. "Do you remember Mr. Hernandez. You say that you lived here a long time ago?" "Certainly," replied she. "He was a very good and true man." Then he noticed in her face an expression of sadness which overshadowed her soul and tortured her.

He did not doubt any longer, and said to her, "You must be my wife, Maria, whom I have not forgotten a single moment, and whom I love with all my soul."

Maria could not restrain her tears, and said, "Yes, I am your wife; rather, I have been your wife; for now, although I should like to call myself so, I am unworthy of loving you. I have lived with a tiger that took me from your side." And she told him all the bitterness and sadness she had endured in the dark abode of that wild beast.

The couple lived united, and loving each other more than in the first years after their marriage. They agreed to take the boy to be baptized; and they called him Juan, and his godfather was the priest of the village. They sent the boy to school; but as soon as his fellows saw him, they made fun of him, and called him Little-Hairy-Body or Juan Tigre. And Juan, who had in his veins the blood of the tiger, with one stroke of his fist by the force of his blow left all those who made fun of him foolish for all their lives. His parents, in order to reform him, left him with his godfather, the priest. He thought he could reform Juan by frightening him by means of the skulls of the dead, which, according to the beliefs of the people, haunted the steeple of the church.

One day, when Juan went up to toll the bells, he saw two skulls, which jumped about as though moved by a mysterious power. Juan smiled, threw them down so that they rolled about, and, when he arrived at home after calling to mass, he said to the priest, "Godfather, your servant-girl is very careless; she left on the stairs of the steeple the two calabashes in which she makes *atole* (cornmeal gruel)." The priest was surprised at the courage of the boy, and replied, saying that he would tell the girl to take better care of her things.

Then he sent him to another town to take a letter to the priest there, with the condition that he should sleep alone in a hut which stood all by itself in the fields. Juan stayed there, as he had been told, continued his way on the following day, and on his way back he slept there again. He had hunger, but had no wood to heat the food that he was carrying.

Juan said to himself, "Why is there no wood or straw of any kind to make a fire, and heat my supper?" At the same moment he heard a noise which announced a falling body. They were bones of skeletons, which Juan used as fuel to heat has meal.

Undoubtedly the ghosts knew his courage, and said, "In the corner which looks southward, at a depth of half a yard, you will find a pot full of gold and silver coin, for, on account of this money, we have been haunting this spot for a long time."

Juan left there, and directed his steps to his godfather, to whom he gave the reply to his message, and explained to him the place that had been indicated to him, and where the money was. The priest took this wealth away in small quantities, so that nobody should know what he was doing.

Two years passed. The father of Juan had come to be rich, because he participated in the enormous wealth that his son had found. He, however, on account of his instincts, had to look for adventures, and make himself famous by his deeds throughout the world.

He left his home, armed only with a goodly iron pole, which he alone, on account of his extraordinary strength, could manage. He met a ghost, a man who carried enormous stones, and a very noted person called "Big-Finger" because he lifted whatever he liked with his first finger and without any effort.

These three wished to fight Juan Tigre; but it was impossible to vanquish him, and he made them his slaves. They traveled about several days, and came to a but in the field which seemed to be inhabited. Notwithstanding appearances, nobody lived there.

The ghost remained there, and was to prepare dinner for his fellows who went out to hunt. Poor ghost! He would better have gone with his friends!

A wildman, ugly, exceedingly ugly, came to the hut, beat him, threw away his dinner, and ordered him to leave at once, or else he would kill him. The hunters came back, and the ghost explained to them what had happened. Then Juan Tigre, the chief, scolded him severely, and ordered that on the following day Big-Finger should stay at home. To him and to Stone-Carrier happened the same as to the ghost.

Then Juan Tigre said, "You all go and hunt, I shall await the wildman and see what he wants." Poor man! Better he had not come!

Yet he did come. Juan beat him so hard, that the poor wildman had to flee precipitately, leaving a line of blood on the road, for Juan Tigre had torn off one of his ears. When Juan's companions arrived, he gave them a good dinner to eat, although they had not been able to provide a meal when it had been their turns.

After dinner they followed the tracks of the wildman, and noted that in all probability he had gone down into a well. They brought halters; and Juan went down to the bottom of the well, telling his companions to pull him up as soon as he should shake the rope. After a few moments Juan shook the rope, and his companions began to pull up something heavy. They were surprised to see a beautiful maiden tied in the halter. They lowered the rope again, and pulled up another, younger girl. The same happened a third time.

Then each one of these bad people said, "This one shall be my wife!" and each one took his future wife by the arm.

They left with their brides and abandoned Juan in the dark well. When the chief saw that the halter was not coming down again, he threatened the wildman with death if he did not take him out of there. All the while, the wildman had been at the bottom of the well, howling on account of the loss of his ear.

The wildman said, "Do not kill me! Let me live here! If you wish for anything, bite my ear which you have, and you will get your wish." Juan bit the ear, and, to his great surprise, he saw himself out of the well without knowing how it had happened.

By means of the ear he also learned the whereabouts of his former companions, who thought Juan would die in the well, and who had taken those beautiful maidens to the house of the King. The King said that he was the ladies' father, and that they had been carried away by a wildman whose whereabouts could not be discovered.

The King compelled his daughters to marry the bad persons who had returned them to their father. They protested, saying that the person who had saved them was a stout, fierce, and ugly man, with whom each of them had left a ring. The father insisted on his idea; and the miserable companions of Juan would have triumphed, if Juan Tigre had not appeared on time at the castle of the King and shown the rings which his daughters had given him.

The King ordered the treacherous friends of Juan to be shot, and said to him, "You shall be the master of my daughters. They love you, because you have saved them from the claws of the monster; and as a prize for your virtues and strength you shall be my heir."

Source: Adapted from "Juan Tigre," Franz Boas, Notes on Mexican Folklore. *Journal of American Folklore* 25 (1912): 241–45.

The Boy Who Became a King

Just as Latino folk culture is often characterized by a synthesis of European and Native American traditions, the following folktale introduces elements of indigenous Yaqui life into a plot that maintains distinctive European features. The quest theme of three brothers seeking their fortunes, the heroine disguised as a man coming to the rescue of her husband or sweetheart, and suitors competing for the hand of a princess are common motifs in European traditional narratives. On the other hand, the setting of the events and the occupations of major characters are localized to the American Southwest. The pattern of extreme contrast set up between the hero's father who judges by surface appearances and the youngest son's father-in-law who judges by accomplishments is typical of the structure in European folktales, also.

Three boys decided to leave their mother and father and go away to work. Their mother made a lunch for each of the boys, and they left. They came to a place where there were some fig trees; here, they ate lunch. At this place the road branched three ways. After lunch, the oldest boy said that he would take the road that went straight ahead. "In one year from now we will meet at this fig tree." The oldest boy cut the tree saying, "When blood comes out of a cut in this tree, it means bad luck; if milk flows, it is good luck."

The oldest boy found good work, and married a fine girl, the daughter of his boss. The next oldest boy married a good girl, and he had good luck. But the youngest encountered very bad luck indeed.

Although the country was full of all kinds of animals, he hunted all day long but found no game for his supper. That night he hunted a place in which he could sleep, and he found a cave. In the cave was a lion. And the lion said to him, "Don't you have any bad luck in your travels about this country?"

"No," said the youngest boy.

The lion then said, "Don't you want to be my captain?"

"Good," said the boy, "but I don't know how to talk your language very well."

"That is all right," answered the lion. "You'll learn soon." The lion took out a horn, blew it, and called all the animals together. When the animals of all the world were there together, the lion talked with them about making this boy their captain. They all said that they would like him for a captain.

Then the lion taught the boy how to talk with every kind of animal. When the boy had been there a month a crow came to see him, and she said, "Listen, my friend, I have two little crows. I want them to be baptized."

"Very well," said the boy. "Bring them here. I will baptize them." So now the boy had two little crow godchildren.

The father crow brought to the boy an egg. "Take this egg, compadre," he said, "and whatever you want, ask the egg for it—it doesn't matter what it is, you'll get it."

So the boy took the egg and set out for a big village. He arrived there very late at night. He took the egg out of his pocket and asked it to make him into a Negro and to give him a guitar. In his black attire, carrying the guitar, he stopped at the house of a lady. He greeted her, "Good evening."

"Good evening, young Negro," she answered.

"I would like to sleep here," he said.

The lady said, "That's all right." She gave him a supper of tortillas, meat, and beans. When he had eaten, she asked him to play and sing. He did. He knew many songs not known to other singers. The lady was so delighted she wanted to dance.

He slept all night on a mat on the floor. Early in the morning the lady arose. She told him to get up. After breakfast she told him to remain there looking after the house while she went out. This lady knew the king in that village very well.

She went to the king and told him that she had a Negro who was very good at playing the guitar and singing.

"Where is he?" asked the king.

"He is in my house." So the king sent a man to bring the young man to him.

This man arrived at the house and said to the boy, "The king wants you." The boy was surprised. "Don't be afraid," said the man. "Let's go."

When the king saw the Negro and heard him play he was very pleased and said, "What size shoe do you wear?"

"Six," he answered. So the king ordered shoes and a whole set of new clothes made for the Negro. Before putting on these new, clean clothes, the young man went to a place where he could bathe himself.

Now, the king had a daughter who was very pretty. This girl wanted to see the boy when he had no clothes on, so she looked through a crack at him when he was bathing. The boy had taken off his outer, black skin and she saw him as a very beautiful boy. She said nothing of this to anyone.

After bathing, the boy put on his black skin and his new clothes and went to supper. Afterwards, the king asked him to sing. He took his guitar and played and sang. They all enjoyed it very much. But the daughter knew about him. She said, "That guitar is old. He should have a new one." The king told the boy that he should have a new guitar.

But the boy said, "No, this is just as good as a new one."

A week later the girl told her father that she would like to get married. So her father sent out notices that he who should have one peso more than the king himself would be allowed to marry his daughter. Many rich dukes came and talked to the king, but not one of them had the necessary wealth. The king was always more wealthy than any of the suitors.

When they had all gone away, the young boy went alone to a small hill outside of the village. Here he took out his egg and talked to it. He said he would like to have a palace, better than all the palaces in the world. Before him, inside the hill arose a palace of pure gold. He then asked for it to be furnished completely with tables and chairs of pure gold. And it was. He ordered pigs and horses to be put in the stables and yards. These also were of gold, and they ate golden grains of corn. The boy went out and commanded that a huge iron gate be put across at the entrance.

Then he went to visit the lady who had taken him to the king. He did not speak of his palace, but said that he had come to see her. She was pleased and asked him to sing for her.

The next day he asked the king, "Why didn't your daughter marry one of those rich men who came here?"

"Because they didn't have any more money than I have," answered the king.

"I have more money than you have," said he.

"Where?" asked the king.

"Do you see that hill over there?" The king thought that there must be a rich mine in the hill.

"Yes, I see the hill," said the king. "Let's go see it closer." The girl wanted to go along too, so the king ordered a big coach for her. They came to the hill and the king said, "Where is your money?"

The young man, dismounting, took out a huge iron key. Everyone was surprised as he went to open the gate. They looked in, then covered their faces with their hands because of the brilliance of the treasure inside. But the girl said to her father, "Go in, go in, go in."

They all entered and saw the palace all made of gold. "Look at my pigs," said the boy. They were also of gold.

"You beat me by one pig!" said the king.

"Let's go see my horses," said the boy. The king did not need more to convince him, but he was always interested in horses, so they went to the stables. The horses were also of gold.

"That's enough. I want to see no more. You can marry my daughter," said the king. The next day the boy married the king's daughter.

The king loved his son-in-law very much. It did not matter if he was a Negro; he was rich. At the wedding everybody danced. The girl danced until she perspired very much. The boy took out a huge handkerchief and wiped her face for her. The next day they went to their palace in the hill.

They were very happy. He talked to her about his two crow godchildren. "But," he said, "I must leave you for a while. It is nearly a year since I left home and I must go see my father."

He ordered ten mules loaded down with money and five men to care for them. The girl warned him that he would have to pass a place where there were many thieves. "Take care," she said, "when you pass that place."

"Very well," he replied, and he set out. The next day he arrived where the thieves were. They asked him to stop and gamble with them. He did, and they won from him all of his mules, with their loads. Next, he lost his fine clothes and had to put on the old clothes of one of the thieves. He sent his five muleteers away, saying there was no more work. Then he set out on foot toward his home.

Since that day had marked a year since he had taken leave of his brothers, he arrived late at the fig tree. He cut the tree, and it indicated good luck by weeping milk. So he went on.

He arrived at his home looking like a vagabond. On seeing him, his parents did not want to admit that he was of their family. His father said to him, "You are no longer my son. Your brothers have done well, but look at you."

That evening they handed him his supper out of the window. They didn't want him in the house. He was told that he could care for the chickens and pigs. If he wanted to stay there, he must sleep in the chicken house.

"Take care that the chickens don't drop on you," said his father.

He went to the chicken house where he was to sleep. When he got there, he talked to the chickens. "If one of you makes a single dropping during the whole night, I'll wring your neck and throw you outside!" he warned them. They all listened attentively.

One chicken said, "This captain is very strict, so be careful."

About midnight, the boy heard a chicken make a dropping. He knew that it was an old, old rooster, but he asked, "Who did that?"

"Not I," said the nearest hen.

"Not I," said the next. And so on down the roost each answered, "Not I." When the question came to the old rooster, he said nothing. The others said that he had done it, and, finally, he admitted it. The boy twisted his neck and threw him outside, a good lesson to the chickens, who did not make a dropping all that night.

The boy's father came the next morning and saw the chicken house clean. "How could this be?" he wondered.

He had some three hundred pigs who were very dangerous and unmanageable. "You are going to take the pigs out today. Be careful, for they are broncos," he said to the boy.

The boy went to the pig sty. There he talked with a big white pig. The pig recognized him as a leader. The boy told this pig to tell the rest of the pigs not to act up that day. And the white pig did so.

The father wanted to count the pigs as they left, so the boy ordered them to pass the gate of the sty in pairs, marching as if in an army. The father was astounded. The pigs marched in pairs out into the country.

The boy said to the white pig, "Tell your companions not to wander far, for I am going to take a nap." They minded him, for they were very contented with their captain. In the afternoon, they returned, marching home to the sty.

The boy thought often of his wife and the golden palace he had left. In a suit at home he had left the crow's egg. After about a month his wife began to wonder what could have happened to her husband.

One day the boy saw a crow flying overhead. "Stop a minute, compadre." he called to the crow. The crow turned about and came back. It was, indeed, his compadre.

"What happened to you?" asked the crow.

The boy told him all that had passed. "If I had paper and pen, I would write to my wife," he added, for he knew how to write very well.

The white pig had a suggestion. He told the crow to fly out to a trash pile and bring back a piece of paper. Then the pig told the crow to pull out a feather. "Make a little hole in the back of my neck and use my blood for ink."

Thus the boy wrote a letter to his wife telling her where the egg was, and asking her to bring it to him.

The crow took the note and flew to the palace of gold. The girl was seated in the door, sadly thinking. She saw the crow fly low over her and suddenly remembered that her husband had a crow compadre. When the crow said "Crak, crak," she called it to come on down. It turned about and brought her the note.

She went to the suit and found the egg in the pocket. She then ordered ten mules loaded with money. She put on clothes of a man, took her pistol, and set out, accompanied by five men. She arrived at the house of the boy's father, where she was received most graciously, for they thought she was a rich man. At dinner the father of the boy talked of the tramp who was caring for the pigs and chickens. He did not know quite what kind of a person he was, for the chickens never soiled the floor of their house at night when this man slept there, and the wild pigs were now very tame and marched like soldiers for him.

The woman, who was dressed as a man, watched at the window and saw the boy come for his dinner. As he went to the chicken house, she joined him. She sat with him while he ate. She said nothing of who she was. "If I show you something I have here, perhaps you will remember me," she said and reached in her pocket and pulled out the handkerchief with which he had wiped her face at their wedding. At that, he recognized his wife. She had brought him a suit of fine clothes, and some women's clothes for herself. They were very happy. They spent the night in the chicken house.

The next morning the father complained that it was very late and that tramp had not yet got up to feed the chickens. He went out and knocked at the door. "Get up!" he said. "The chickens are hungry and it is late."

"Excuse me a moment, I'll be out in a little while," the boy answered.

At last he and his wife appeared, dressed in all their finery.

The old man said, "Of course, of course, you are my son."

But the boy, by means of the egg, destroyed his father, the house and everything but the animals. With his wife he went home to their palace of gold in the hill.

Source: Adapted from "Yaqui Myths and Legends." Ruth Warner Giddings. 1959, Copyright not registered or renewed, pp. 69–78. August 24, 2008. Available online http://www.sacred-texts.com/nam/sw/yml/index.htm.

Maria the Ash Girl

Beginning in the latter decades of the twentieth century, Chileans immigrated to the United States in increasing numbers. As is the case with much Latino folklore, Chilean folktale repertoires have been enriched by both Native American and European traditions. The following version of the tale most widely known as "Cinderella" closely resembles Spanish versions of the same tale that date back to the period of Spanish exploration of the Western Hemisphere. The opening proverb is a formulaic phrase used to open tales in this folk culture; the purpose is similar to the use in English fairy tales of the phrase, "Once upon a time."

"To tell, one must know, and to know, one must listen."

Once upon a time was a man, who had a daughter named Maria. Not far away was a neighbor, to whose house Maria went daily after embers to light the fire, and who used to give her sops [a piece of food dipped in liquid] soaked in honey. One day she said, "Tell your father to marry me, and I will always give you sops in honey."

Maria went to her father and said, "Father, marry our neighbor, for she is good to me, and gives me honeyed sops."

But her father said: "No, Maria; now she gives you sops, but by and by she will give you gall." However, at last her father said that he would marry the neighbor, but she was not to complain if she found herself ill treated. The neighbor had a daughter, also named Maria, who was of the same age. The father married the neighbor, who directly began to abuse Maria, because she was prettier than her own girl. She slapped her face, thrust her into the kitchen with soiled clothing, and called her Ash-girl.

Now, Maria had a heifer, with which she amused herself all day long; and the crone, who was jealous, besought her husband to give her own child a heifer too. As if that was not enough, she told Maria to kill it, because she did no work, but played with it all day. The father thought it hard, but was obliged to consent, for fear that his wife would make it worse for Maria. So the crone called her, and said, "Tomorrow you must have the heifer killed, for you are a lazybones, and do nothing but amuse yourself."

Then the girl took to kissing the heifer, who said, "Maria, don't cry; when they kill me, beg leave to let you wash my heart and liver, where you will find a wand of virtue, which will give you all you desire. Take care of it, and conceal it in your belt, so that it may not be seen." The next day they killed the heifer, and Maria went to the river to wash the heart, where she found a wand. When she had done, and put the parts in a jar, it floated down stream. She burst out crying, for she was sure that her stepmother would beat her; and while she was weeping, up came an old woman with a blue dress, who said: "Maria, why do you cry?"

"How can I help crying? My jar has floated away with the pieces I washed, and when my stepmother knows, she will beat me to death."

"Do not cry," said the woman; "go to yonder but at the water's edge and sleep, while I get the pieces." Maria went to the hut, but instead of resting she swept the room, made a fire, and got supper; after that, she went to sleep. Soon there was a knock, and when she opened the door, there stood the jar; she took it, and went home. "Why so late?" asked her stepmother. Maria said that the jar had floated off, and that an old woman had gone to look for it while she slept in a hut; when she awoke, it was at the door. "What is that on your forehead?" said the crone.

"I do not know," answered the girl. They brought a mirror, and when she looked, she saw that she had a star on her forehead. Her stepmother tried to rub it away, but the more she scoured, the sweeter and brighter grew the star. So they made her wear a bandage, that none might perceive how superior she was.

The other Maria said to the crone, "Mother, bid them kill my heifer, and I will go wash the pieces, so that I may get a star on my forehead, like the ash-girl." Her mother bade it be killed, and the girl went to the river to wash; when she was done, the jar floated away, and she pretended to be grieved.

The old woman in blue came and asked: "Why do you cry, my child?"

"How can I help crying? My jar has floated down the stream." The stranger answered: "Sleep in yonder hut, and when you wake, you will find the jar."

The girl went in a rage, and said: "How, sleep in this dirty cabin, I?" She waited in disdain, and after a while rose, opened the door, and found her jar; she took it and went home. When her mother saw her, she said: "Maria, what is that on your forehead?" They brought a mirror, and when she looked she saw that it was the wattles of a turkey gobbler. Her mother tried to take it away, but the more she pulled the larger and uglier it became, so that at last, not knowing what else to do, she covered it up with a piece of silk. One day there was a dance at court, which Maria desired to attend; she drew out her wand, and asked for clothes, a coach and servants, and all that was needful to go as a fine lady. Presently she found before her beautiful clothes, with whatever else she wanted; and when she put them on, if she was pretty before, she was prettier now

While the rest were asleep, she went to the dance, and as she arrived, there was such applause that the king's son came forth to see. The hall was illumined with the star she had on her brow, and when the prince saw, he was so charmed that all night long he would dance with no one else. When it was time to go, she jumped into her coach in such haste that she dropped one of her glass slippers; the prince could not overtake her, but only kept the shoe.

The next day, he bade his servants search the town and bring the lady, so that he might marry her. They went from house to house, but could find no one whom the slipper fitted. When they came to the house her stepmother bade her daughter bind up her feet, so that she might make them small enough to put on the slipper and marry the prince; lest Maria should be seen, they hid her behind a tub.

Now the crone's daughter had a parrot, and when the men came to try on the shoe, it cried out: "Ha, ha! It's Turkey-crest who's standing there; for Star-on-brow look behind the tub!"

After it had shrieked this many times, they said: "Let us see what the parrot is talking about," and when they looked behind the tub, there was Maria. They made her come out and try the slipper, which fitted perfectly, while everyone perceived here was the lady who had been at the ball. They conducted her to the prince, in spite of all the crone's fuss; the prince married her, and there was a royal wedding which lasted a long time; so ends the story.

Source: Adapted from "Filipino (Tagalog) Versions of Cinderella." Fletcher Gardner and W. W. Newell, *Journal of American Folklore* 19 (1906): 265–280, pp. 273–275.

Blanca Flor

The story of "Blanca Flor" (White Flower), collected during oral performance in the West Texas–Mexico border region, displays the influence of European tradition on the Latino folktales of Texas and northern Mexico. The narrative is obviously a variant of the well-known "Snow White and the Seven Dwarves," popularized in children's literature and a Disney film of the same name, but the content does not suggest any pop culture influence. The effects of Roman Catholicism, however, appear in the cloistering of Blanca Flor's sleeping body in a chapel and in the role of a corrupt sexton (in Roman Catholicism, an individual charged with minor secular duties related to the maintenance of the church property) in freeing Flor Blanca from her enchantment.

Long ago there lived a queen who was as beautiful as she was vain. This queen had a little daughter named Blanca Flor who was also very beautiful, and grew more so every day.

The queen, to satisfy her vanity, had a magic mirror which she consulted daily, asking it always, "Who is the most beautiful woman in the world?"

And the mirror would answer. "You, and you alone."

As the years went by, Blanca Flor's beauty increased daily. One day, the queen asked her mirror the usual question, but it answered, "Blanca Flor."

The queen, amazed at the mirror's answer, asked again, "Mirror, who is the most beautiful woman in the world?"

And the mirror answered again, "Your daughter, Blanca Flor."

The queen, who was cruel and spiteful, was angry, and decided to have Blanca Flor killed.

She called a trusted servant who had oftentimes carried out her evil orders, and she said to him, "Juan, Blanca Flor must be killed."

"But your Majesty . . . ," said the servant in surprise.

"Not a word more!" exclaimed the queen. "Tomorrow, early, I want you to take Blanca Flor into the forest and there kill her. I also want proof of your obedience."

The next day Juan invited Blanca Flor to cut flowers in the forest. While they walked, Juan was filled with pity for the maiden and, unable to bear the thought of what he had to do to her, he told Blanca Flor all. "My princess, your mother has ordered me to kill you. Since you have always been good and kind to me, I can't harm you. Nevertheless, if I return to the palace without proof of your death, the queen will order my execution. However, I have thought of a way in which we may fool the queen. Give me some of your garments; I will kill a rabbit and with its blood stain them. Then I will take them to the queen."

When he had done all this, Juan told Blanca Flor, "Now, go with God."

Blanca Flor thanked Juan; then she walked deeper into the forest. As the day came to an end, she began to hear the night creatures stirring. With each step she took, the fear of these beasts increased. Suddenly, she saw a light. Blanca Flor ran towards it and soon came to a grass-thatched hut. The princess knocked on the door but nobody answered. She knocked again; nobody answered. Fear made her open the door and go into the hut, and there in the middle of the room was a table set with food and drink. Blanca Flor was so hungry that, sitting down at the table, she first ate; then gave thanks to God. The food made her drowsy, so she stretched out near the stove and went to sleep.

The hut which Blanca Flor had found belonged to a band of robbers. At dawn the highwaymen arrived, and imagine their surprise on finding a young and beautiful girl asleep near the stove in their house.

The noise the bandits made awoke Blanca Flor.

"Don't be afraid, girl," said the robber-chief. "We won't harm you."

The chief meant this. The highwaymen were kindhearted and stole only from the rich to give to the poor.

When Blanca Flor saw that the thieves were good and kindhearted, she told them of her mother's cruelty.

"You can stay here with us," said the robber-chief. "We already know how cruel the queen is. But be careful, for if she finds out that you are alive, she will again try to kill you."

Meanwhile, Juan had returned to the palace. There he showed the queen the bloodstained garments. Oh! the queen was so happy with this proof of Blanca Flor's death. She rewarded Juan lavishly.

That night in her bedroom the queen consulted her magic mirror. "Magic mirror, who is the most beautiful woman in the world?"

And the mirror answered, "Your daughter Blanca Flor."

Pale with anger, the queen called the guards and ordered them to bring Juan immediately.

"Juan," said the queen, "You have lied to me. Blanca Flor is alive."

"But your majesty ..." began Juan. Before he could continue, the queen launched herself on the poor man and stabbed him to death on the spot.

That night the queen could not sleep, thinking of how she could find Blanca Flor and kill her.

The following day the queen disguised herself as a peasant, altering her face with magic creams and so changing her looks that nobody recognized her. Then, in a cunningly carved silver coffer, she placed an enchanted golden necklace. Anyone who wore this necklace would immediately fall into a death-like sleep.

The queen left the palace and soon came to the forest. She walked into the woods and at last arrived at the hut where Blanca Flor was living.

The girl was alone in the hut when she heard a knock at the door. She looked out of the window and saw a sweet old lady. Thinking the old woman was harmless, she opened the door.

"Child," said the old queen, "I wish you would be kind enough to give me a glass of water. I'm very tired and very thirsty."

"Come in, Señora," answered Blanca Flor, and running into the kitchen she brought the glass of water.

The queen drank the water, thanked Blanca Flor, and said, "Niña, I have to go now, but since you have been so kind, I am going to give you this golden necklace."

"Thank you, Señora," said Blanca Flor, taking the necklace and placing it around her throat. As soon as Blanca Flor fastened the clasp, she fell to the floor as if dead.

Leaving her daughter right where she had fallen, the evil queen fled back to her palace.

That evening when the thieves returned they found Blanca Flor seemingly dead. They did all they could to revive the girl, but all their attempts were useless.

The bandits loved Blanca Flor so much that they decided to build a crystal coffin for her. This the robbers then placed in a cave that was near the hut so that they could go and see Blanca Flor every day.

Time passed and one very rainy day a prince took refuge from the weather in the cave where Blanca Flor was lying. When the prince's servants lit torches, they saw Blanca Flor in her crystal coffin. Immediately, the prince fell in love with her. He thought that the beautiful girl was dead, but ordered that the coffin be taken to his kingdom. There he built a beautiful chapel and in it placed Blanca Flor.

One day the sexton in charge of Blanca Flor's chapel fell sick and another took his place. The new one liked to steal things, and seeing the magic necklace, he decided to take it.

Very carefully the new sexton removed the necklace from Blanca Flor. A thunderclap was heard and she awoke. The sexton, terrified, ran out screaming. Hearing all this noise, the prince ran to the chapel, where he found Blanca Flor sitting in her coffin. The girl, when she saw the prince, fell in love with him.

Blanca Flor told the prince all that happened to her. The prince then raised an army and went and punished Blanca Flor's mother.

Then Blanca Flor and the prince were married and lived happily ever after.

Source: "Blanca Flor," Gabriel A. Cordova Jr. *Magic Tales of Mexico.* M.A. Thesis. Texas Western College, El Paso, TX http://www.genecowan.com/magictales/home.html, retrieved August 6, 2008.

The Bear Prince

Most readers will note similarities between the plot of "The Bear Prince" and the classic European folktale of "Beauty and the Beast," for example, a father's violation of a forbidden realm, the exchange of a daughter's in marriage to the owner of the realm, and the husband who appears to be a loathsome beast. As is the case with "The Little Green Rabbit," Roman Catholicism is an important factor in the tale; the protagonist, Ninfa, will only consent to marriage to the Bear Prince if they are "married according to Catholic rites." The pious Catholic heroine is matched against a witch antagonist, but triumphs due to her strength of character. This assertive female character is another similarity to "The Little Green Rabbit." The common element may be due to the fact that both tales were collected from female narrators. That cause, however, is difficult to establish; therefore, this explanation must be considered speculative

Once upon a time there was a very poor woodcutter who had three beautiful daughters. Of the three girls, the youngest was the most beautiful. One day the woodcutter went into the forest and was chopping down an oak tree when a very large and horrible bear wrenched the axe from his hands.

"Who gave you permission to cut the wood in my forest?" growled the bear. "You have been stealing my timber and now you must pay for it with your life."

"Please forgive me, *Señor Oso,*" said the poor woodcutter, "I was only cutting the wood to sell it and thus support my three little daughters. If you kill me, my little girls will starve."

The Bear remained thoughtful and then said, "There is only one way in which you life may be saved. You have to give me one of your daughters in marriage."

The woodcutter did not know what to say or do. Finally the thought of dying and leaving his daughters destitute forced him to agree to the Bear's proposal.

The woodcutter returned home and told his daughters what had happened.

"Father," said the two eldest girls, "we would rather die than marry that Bear."

Ninfa, the youngest, said. "Father, I will marry the Bear."

Next day, Ninfa and her father went into the forest where the Bear was waiting for them. After seeing the beautiful maiden, he was satisfied.

Ninfa, however, said to the Bear, "*Señor Oso,* my mother always taught me that in all things I should always follow God's law. If I must marry you, I want to be married according to the Catholic rites."

The Bear agreed, provided a priest could come to the forest. The woodcutter went in search of a priest and soon returned with one. Ninfa and the Bear were then married.

The Bear took Ninfa to his cave, and when it grew dark he chanted:

Bear so hairy, Bear so alarming,
Change into a prince handsome and charming.

In an instant the Bear changed into a handsome prince. He then told Ninfa, "I am an enchanted prince, cursed by a witch into being a bear by day and a man by night. You do anything you want around here on one condition, that you never reveal that I am an enchanted prince."

Ninfa, happily promised that she would never reveal the secret.

The next morning they arose from bed, and the prince said:

Prince so handsome, prince so charming,
Change into a Bear, hairy and alarming.

In an instant the prince had changed back into a bear.

Days followed days and Ninfa felt a desire to go and visit her family in the village. However, she did not know how to ask the prince for permission. Finally, she mustered enough courage and said to him.

"Aside from you, husband, I don't have anyone with whom to talk. I wish you would let me go to the village to see my father and sisters. It isn't far, and if I leave early enough I will be back before it gets dark."

The prince did not want to let Ninfa go, but the girl insisted so much that he finally consented. However, he make her repeat her oath never to reveal the prince's secret.

Next day Ninfa got up early. She dressed herself richly and went to see her father and sisters, who welcomed her joyously. However, the devil, who never sleeps, soon filled the sisters with envy. They began to poke fun at Ninfa, jealous of the fact that she was wearing rich jewels and costly garments.

"You married a bear, what shame!" the sisters repeatedly told her.

So many times did the sisters repeat this, that finally Ninfa lost her temper and revealed her husband's secret. The sisters were deeply amazed to hear Ninfa's tale.

The eldest one then said, "Look, Ninfa, why don't you disenchant the prince? What you have to do is easy. Get him drunk tonight. When he goes to sleep, tie him up and gag him. As soon as day breaks and the prince wakes up, he will not be able to say the magic words, and the enchantment will be broken. Then you will have a husband with a human form forever."

Ninfa returned to the bear's cave and that night did everything her sister had suggested. The prince awoke the next morning, and imagine his surprise at finding himself tied and gagged!

He could not say the magic rhyme and the enchantment was broken.

"Wife," the prince later said to Ninfa, "you have broken your promise; now you must bear the consequences. To break the enchantment and live happily ever after, we two had to live happily married a year and a day. Since you have disobeyed me, you are going to have to look for me. You will not find me until you locate the Castle of Faith."

Saying this, the prince vanished and Ninfa was left alone. She cried and was sorry, for she truly loved the prince. Then, determined to be reunited with her husband, Ninfa decided to go and look for the Castle of Faith. Tying a few belongings together, she slung them on her back and left on her search.

She walked and walked and finally arrived at a forest where a wizard lived.

"*Niña*," said the wizard, "what do you want here in this forest?"

"I am looking for the Castle of Faith," answered Ninfa, "do you happen to know where it is?"

"I don't know where that castle is located." said the wizard, "but follow this road until you reach my father's house. He may know where the castle is. Take this nut, and if you ever find yourself in trouble break it."

Ninfa thanked the old man, and left, finally reaching the house where the wizard's father lived. She asked him if he knew where the Castle of Faith was.

The old man did not know but said, "Look, walk along this road until you come to the house of my eldest brother. He has traveled much, perhaps he can tell you where the castle is. I am going to give you another nut just as my son did. If you find yourself in trouble, break it and it will help you."

Ninfa walked and walked and finally came to the house of the third wizard. He also did not know where the castle was. However, he told her what to do, "The Moon probably knows. Follow this road and soon you will come to her house. But be careful, the Moon may be angry. I am also going to give you a nut. If you find yourself in trouble, break it."

Ninfa left. The poor girl was very, very tired, but at last that night she arrived at the moon's house. She knocked on the door and a little old lady, who was the moon's housekeeper, came out.

"Merciful God! Daughter, what are you doing here?" asked the old lady. "Don't you know that if the Moon finds you here she will eat you?"

Ninfa tearfully told the old woman all that had happened.

"Look," said the old one, "you hide behind the stove. When the moon comes, I will carelessly ask her if she knows where the castle is."

At dawn the moon came in, angry because she had stuck in her finger a thorn from a prickly pear cactus.

The moon came into the kitchen and said, "Human flesh I smell here. Give it to me, or on you I will feast."

"Go on," said the old woman, "you're crazy. Just because there is a roast in the oven, you think it's human flesh. Sit down and eat so that you can go to bed. You are very tired."

The moon sat down to eat and the old lady began to talk. "The other day an owl went by, and I got to talking with her. She told me she had heard talk about the Castle of Faith. You, who know so many things, surely know where this castle is."

"To tell you the truth," said the Moon, "I don't know. The one who probably knows is the Sun."

The moon went to bed and the little old lady whispered to Ninfa, "Quickly, leave before the Moon wakes up. Go along this road and soon you will arrive at the house of the Sun."

Ninfa left and she walked and walked, until finally she came to the Sun's house. She knocked on the door and another little old lady answered.

"*Valgame Dios, niña!* [God save me, child!]" she exclaimed, "What are you doing here?" Don't you know that if the Sun finds you here he will burn you?"

Ninfa began to cry, and between sobs told her story to the little old lady. They were both gloomily talking when the house suddenly filled with light and the Sun came in. Poor Ninfa. She crossed herself and prepared to die.

But the little old lady yelled, "Wait, Sun! Wait! This poor child is looking for the Castle of Faith."

"Ah!" exclaimed the Sun, "so you are looking for the Castle of Faith."

Tearfully Ninfa told the Sun what had happened to her.

"I know where the castle is," said the Sun. "But it is very far from here. I could take you, but it is getting late and you know that I am not allowed to go out after dark. But look! Near here lives my good friend, *El Aire*, the Wind. He can take you. You walk along this path and when you get to *El Aire's* home, you tell him that it was I who sent you."

Ninfa left and, after walking a good while, arrived at the Wind's house. She knocked and the Wind screamed, "Come in whoever it is!"

Ninfa entered and told *El Aire* that the Sun had sent her with a request.

"Granted," said *El Aire,* "no matter what it may be."

She told *Senor Aire* all that had adversely happened to her and that she wanted to go to the Castle of Faith.

"Do not worry," said *El Aire*, "I, myself, will take you."

Ninfa straddled *El Aire's* back, and in less time than it takes to wink an eye, they arrived at the castle.

"Look," said *El Aire,* "it seems that there is a fiesta in the castle."

The whole castle was brilliantly lit and the sound of violins and guitars could be heard everywhere.

"I have to leave," he told Ninfa. "With the help of God, everything will come out all right."

And turning into a whirlwind, he rushed away.

Ninfa knocked on the door of the castle, and a servant come out. "In what may I serve you?" asked the servant.

"I would like to see the prince."

"*Señora*," answered the servant, "you cannot see him at this moment. He just got married and now is dancing with the new princess."

"Well, if that is the case, Senor, at least let me come in and see this *baile* [dance]. I have never seen such a magnificent *baile*."

The servant told Ninfa, "I am going to let you come in, but one condition, that you be careful and not let the bride see you. Since you have not been invited, the bride would be angry at seeing you here."

Ninfa entered the castle and saw her husband, the prince, eating at a table and surrounded by his guests.

She flattened herself against the wall. From there she began trying to attract the prince's attention. He kept on talking; he had not seen the poor girl.

Ninfa tried so hard to get the prince's attention that the bride saw her. She was an evil witch who with her magic had blinded the prince and made him marry her.

The prince then saw Ninfa and recognized her immediately. He yelled at the servants. telling them to bring Ninfa to him, but with the noise nobody heard him.

The witch screamed at her servants, "Run that beggar out!"

The servants were about to lay their hands on Ninfa when the girl broke one of the magic nuts the wizards had given her. In an instant Ninfa turned into a little rat which ran hither and yon. When the witch saw this, she turned into a huge cat which began to chase the rat. The rat sprang atop the prince's table, and onto his plate. There Ninfa broke another nut and turned into a grain of rice which became lost among many on the prince's plate. The cat also jumped on the table, turning instantly into a chicken which began to eat the rice.

Ninfa then broke the other nut and turned into a coyote which ate the chicken in one bite.

Ninfa then was transformed back into human form to be reunited with the prince and both lived happily ever after.

Source: "The Bear Prince," Gabriel A. Cordova Jr. *Magic Tales of Mexico.* M.A. Thesis. Texas Western College, El Paso, TX. http://www.genecowan.com/magic-tales/home.html, retrieved August 6, 2008.

The Prohibited Chamber

The following tale of a clever young woman who uses her wits to escape death at the hands of her future husband is most widely recognized as the "Bluebeard" plot. Folklorist Gabriel A. Cordova Jr. notes that while this tale, and related plots involving the victimization of a naïve young woman by a suitor, is popular in British, Anglo-American, and Scandinavian traditions, it is relatively rare in Latin America. The capture of girls by means of hypnotism rather than enchantment is a modern adaptation.

Once there was an evil wizard who, dressed as a beggar, would go from house to house asking for alms and would steal the prettiest girls he could find. None of them could ever return home.

One day he knocked on the door of a house where lived a man with three beautiful daughters. The eldest opened the door and gave him a piece of bread.

When she gave it to him he touched her arm and hypnotized her. Then he made her enter the basket that he always carried on his back and took her to his house which was situated in the midst of the woods. Everything there was magnificent, and she had everything she could wish for.

After a few days the wizard told her that he had to go on a journey, that he would leave her the keys to all the house, and that she could enter every room except one. If she should enter that room she would surely die. Also, he gave her an egg and asked her to take good care of it.

As soon as the wizard was out of sight, the girl looked into every room and found beautiful things that delighted her. At last, she approached the prohibited chamber, and after a moment's indecision, her curiosity won and she entered the room.

What she saw made her tremble. There were hundreds of girls that had been kidnapped and all looked as if they had fallen asleep. The girl, frightened at the sight, went running out of the room as fast as she could.

In her haste, she dropped the egg that she carried in her hand, but it did not break. When she picked it up she noticed that the egg had turned red, and although she tried to clean it, the egg stayed red.

After some time the wizard came back. He noticed what had happened to the egg, struck the girl, and dragged her into the prohibited chamber, where he left her with the others.

58 Latino American Folktales

The wizard then went back to the same house and stole the second sister and the same thing happened to her.

He went back a third time and kidnapped the younger sister, but this sister was very wise. When the wizard gave her the keys and the egg, she took the egg and deposited it in the cupboard. Then she took the keys and went into the prohibited chamber. She was amazed at seeing so many girls lying as if in a profound sleep. Amongst them she recognized her two sisters.

She left the room and closed the door. When she heard the wizard returning, she took the egg and the keys and went to meet him.

"You shall be my wife because you have resisted curiosity," he exclaimed.

As the girl had broken the spell, the wizard had lost his power and she could do with him as she pleased, so she went to the prohibited chamber and awoke all the girls. Then she went to the wizard and told him, "Before I marry you, you must go and take a basket full of gold to my parents."

She took a great big basket and in it she hid her two sisters covering them with pieces of gold. Then she told the wizard to take the basket but not to stop on the road because she would be watching him from the window.

The man took the basket and started walking but soon was worn out by fatigue. He sat down to rest, but immediately heard a voice which said, "I am watching you from my window." Thinking it was the voice of his future wife, he got up and walked a while longer. Every time he tried to rest, the same thing happened, until finally he reached the house where his fiancée's parents lived. There he left the basket.

In the meantime, his future wife took a piece of cardboard and made a head which she placed on the window sill of the second floor, making it look as if someone was watching from the window. Then she went and let out the other victims and invited them all to her wedding. Finally, she covered her whole body with feathers, disguising herself as a rare bird so that no one could recognize her, and left the house. Soon she met some of the guests that she had invited to the wedding and they asked her, "From where do you come beautiful bird?"

"From the house where the wizard is being wedded."

"And please tell, what does the beautiful bride do?"

"After being all dressed up in her beautiful wedding gown she leans out of the window looking down."

When the wizard returned home, the window of the second floor was open, he looked towards it and saw the head there. He thought it was his future wife and he ran excitedly into the house, but upon entering he encountered all the family and sisters of the girl, who dragged him into the chamber, locked the door and set fire to the house.

And this was the end of the wizard and his prohibited chamber.

Source: "The Prohibited Chamber," Gabriel A. Cordova Jr. *Magic Tales of Mexico.* M.A. Thesis. Texas Western College, El Paso, TX. 1951. http://www.genecowan.com/magictales/, retrieved August 6, 2008.

Tale of the Rabbit

Mexico was the birthplace of some of the most advanced cultures in the Western Hemisphere (see, for example, "Quetzalcoatl and Tezcat-lipoca"). With the Spanish conquest in the 1500s, European influence extended into the traditional folktale repertoire. The "Tale of the Rabbit," actually a tale cycle (a group of related tales about the same character), attests to the fact that the narrative is a European and Native American blending. While Spanish is the language in which tales such as this are transmitted and Latino folktales may rely heavily on Spanish sources, the character of trickster Coyote is widely distributed throughout the folklore of Western and Southwestern Native America. The following tale is particularly interesting for its inclusion of the "Tar Baby" incident (in the form of little wax monkeys), a motif that is commonly associated with African American traditions. Any explanation for the presence of Tar Baby in this narrative must remain speculative, however. Most of the other episodes of Rabbit's adventures are common in European folktales, however. In the last episode of this cycle Rabbit suffers a fate similar to that imposed on his victims. This moralistic ending is unusual.

There was a woman who had a *chile* pepper garden; and every day she went to watch it, because the Rabbit ate much of it. One day she went, and on the road met an *arriera* [a species of ant], and asked her if she did not know how to prevent the Rabbit from eating the *chile* peppers. The *arriera* replied that she did not know, and that she should ask her sister the *barendera* [a species of ant], who came behind. The woman met the *barendera,* and asked her. Then the ant said that she should make four little monkeys of wax, and that she should nail them up in the opening in the wall where the Rabbit entered, two on each side, and that she should go the next day to see if the Rabbit had fallen into the trap.

She placed the four little monkeys of wax; and the Rabbit arrived, and said to them, "See here, monkey of wax? If you do not let me pass, I'll box your ears;" and he boxed the little wax monkey's ears, and Rabbit's little hand stuck fast.

He said again, "Look here, little monkey of wax! If you don't let me pass, I have another hand, and I'll box your ears again"; and he boxed his ears, and the other little hand stuck fast.

He said again, "Look here, little monkey of wax! If you do not let go of my little hands, I'll kick you!" and he kicked him, and his little foot stuck fast.

He said again, "Look here, little monkey of wax! If you don't let go of my hands and of my foot, I'll kick you again. I have another little foot."

They were talking thus when the good woman arrived, and said to him, "Ah, it must be you who eats my *chile* peppers. Now you'll pay for what you have done to me." She put him in a net which she was carrying, and took him to her house.

When she got to her house, she hung him up in the middle of the house, and said, "What shall I do with you?" She thought she would throw boiling water over him; but the lady had no water, and went to fetch it and left the door locked.

The Rabbit was still hanging in the net; but since the house stood by the roadside, it so happened that a Coyote passed by, and the Rabbit, as soon as he saw the Coyote, began to talk, to speak, and said, "How can they want to marry me by force, me, who is so small, and I do not want to marry!"

Then the Coyote drew near, and asked him what he was saying; and Rabbit spoke to him, asking the Coyote if he would not place himself in that net, for he himself was caught in the net because they wanted to marry him to a pretty girl, and he did not want to marry. Then the Coyote said to him that he accepted what the Rabbit proposed. The Coyote placed himself in the net, and the Rabbit escaped.

When the dear old woman found the Coyote, she said to him, "Ah, how did the Rabbit turn into a Coyote!" put the pot of water over the fire, and, when it was boiling, she threw it over the Coyote. The Coyote was burnt, but only his backside was burnt. Then the Coyote left, rolling himself on the road, but the Rabbit had escaped to hide in a "dragon fruit" cactus patch.

When the Coyote passed by, the Rabbit said to him, "Good day, Uncle Coyote!"

Then, the Coyote turned to see who spoke to him, and the Coyote said, "Why did you deceive me?"

And the Rabbit replied, "Because they did not find me, they punished you; but really I was about to marry a girl."

Then Rabbit said to Coyote, "Let us not quarrel. Better let us eat dragon fruit," and threw one down from above. Rabbit said to Coyote, "Shut your eyes and open your mouth!" He threw one down, and then another one. The two were clean; but the third one he did not clean, but threw it down with all the spines on it. The Coyote caught it in his mouth and when the spines pierced his tongue he rolled about, and the Rabbit ran away.

While the Coyote was rolling in pain, Rabbit found a wasps' nest, put it in a cradle and covered it with a blanket. The buzzing of the insects was loud and soon the Coyote cam to investigate. When Rabbit saw the Coyote pass by, he said to him, "Coyote, burnt backsides!"

The Coyote said, "What do you say to me?"

Rabbit replied, "I say to you, that you should come and help me rock my little sister, who is crying, and my mother is not here."

The Coyote did not reply to this. "You owe me much. You deceived me, saying that I was going to marry, and then you threw me a dragon fruit with spines, and now I'll take revenge for what you have done to me."

The Rabbit said to him, "But I do not know you, and have never seen you. Maybe those are others, perhaps my brothers."

And the Coyote said to him, "Then you have brothers?"

"Certainly," he said to him. "Man alive, who knows which one that may be who wronged you so!"

"And you, what are you doing here?"

"My mother has been away a long time to get *tortillas* to eat, and left me here rocking this little girl. Now I wish that you would stay here in my place, while I go to look for her, that she may come. When she returns, she will give you tortillas also" The Coyote stayed there with the wasps' nest in the cradle.

When the Rabbit left, he said to Coyote, "If you see that my sister does not stop crying, box her ears and leave her."

The Coyote did so. He got tired of rocking the cradle, and the noise did not stop. He boxed her ears with vigor, and out came a swarm of wasps, who gave the Coyote a good dose of stinging and flew away.

The Coyote followed the road, and said to himself, "Where shall I find the Rabbit?" He walked along the road.

The Rabbit spoke to him, and said, "Coyote, burnt backsides?" and the Coyote asked him what he was saying.

The Rabbit said to him that he was asking him to help him pull out a cheese that was there. The Rabbit was in a pond, and the moon was shining and was seen reflected in the water, and this looked like the cheese which the Rabbit said he was pulling out. The Rabbit left the Coyote there, saying that he was going to rest for a while, because he was very tired. The Coyote began to pull at the cheese; but since it was only a reflection in the water he could never grasp it. Finally, he got tired and went on his way.

After that he walked along the road, when he passed by the place Rabbit had stopped a picked up a large stone. The Rabbit spoke to him, and said, "Good day, Uncle Coyote!"

The Coyote said to him, "Now you won't escape me, for you have deceived me much." "No," said the Rabbit to him, "it is not I. Since the world has existed I have been forced to remain here in this place, with this stone in my hand;" for the Rabbit, as soon as he had seen the Coyote, put the large stone into his hand. He said that he had been left right there supporting that stone, for, if he let go of it, the world would be lost.

The Coyote believed him; and the Rabbit said to him, "Sir, will you not help me a little while with this stone, for I am very tired?"

The Coyote took the stone. The Rabbit said to him, "Uncle Coyote, sir? Don't let go of the stone, else the world will be lost."

The Rabbit went away, saying to the Coyote that he would soon return; but the Rabbit did not come back. He went on; and the Coyote, who soon grew tired, let the stone down gradually, and looked at the sky to see if it was coming down. But when he looked and saw that it was not so, he let the stone down until he put it down on the ground.

He left it and went along his way and said, "Whenever I find the Rabbit, I must kill him, because he has fooled me too much."

The Rabbit placed himself by the wayside, among the reeds. When the Coyote passed by, the Rabbit held a guitar, which, as soon as he saw the Coyote, he began to play, and said, "Good day, Uncle Coyote!"

The Coyote said to him, "Come down, that we may talk together!"

"No, Uncle Coyote! Indeed, sir, you are much annoyed with me."

The Coyote said to him, "You have deceived me much, and therefore I am annoyed." "No, Uncle Coyote," he said to him, " I am the best one of all, and, sir, don't be annoyed with me. I know well what has happened, but I did not do those things. My brother, he is a very bad one; it is he who has done all these things. But now he is about to marry, and I am waiting for the wedding party. They have been delayed a very long time. Who knows what they are doing! I should like to go and look for them if you would stay here and play the guitar; I'll give you a sign, sir, when the bridal couple is coming. I'll fire some rockets, so that you may know it, sir; and then you must play more strongly, so that they can dance when they come."

The Coyote did so. The Rabbit went. After a little while the Rabbit came and set fire to the reeds. The Coyote, believing that the bridal couple was coming, continued to play and began to dance. Before he knew it, he was in the midst of the flames. He could not escape; and the poor Coyote was burnt, and died.

The Rabbit came to look, and mourned the death of the Coyote, and said to himself, "Poor Uncle Coyote! Now he is dead, indeed, and where shall I go now?"

The Rabbit went to the bank of a river. He could not cross the river, and began to say, "Whoever takes me across may eat me."

He was saying thus, when. the Alligator came, and said to him, "I'll take you across." "Well!" said the Rabbit. He climbed up on the back of the Alligator.

When he came near the other bank, the Alligator said to him, "Now I am going to eat you."

"And don't you feel any pity," replied the Rabbit, "to eat such a little fatty as myself?" The Alligator said, "What shall we do?"

"Let us go nearer the bank," replied the Rabbit, "that you may eat me easily, sir." Already they were on the bank. The Rabbit said to the Alligator, "Does it not seem to you, sir, that there are some large leaves there? I'll fetch them; and then I shall throw myself down on them for you to use as a plate that you may not lose anything."

The Alligator agreed. The Rabbit went—and never came back.

On the other side there were old stubbles; and the Rabbit found only a little piece of field. This gave him an idea. He thought, "Now that I have a field, I can say I have grown a crop of corn. I'll sell much corn, and to whom shall I sell it? I'll sell one bushel to Aunt Cockroach, another one to Aunt Hen, one to Uncle Dog, one to Uncle Lion, and one to Uncle Hunter."

The Rabbit had a little ranch, and when he went out to take a walk, he used to lock the door of the house. Since, however, he had fooled the Alligator and owed him his life, the Rabbit was on his guard. When he arrived, he said, "Good day, dear House!" The House never replied.

After a time the Alligator informed himself as to where Rabbit lived, and went to place himself near his bed, that he might eat the Rabbit when he arrived.

On that day when Rabbit returned home he said, "Good day, dear House!"

The Alligator replied, "Good day, Rabbit!"

"What? You never answer me, dear House!" He opened the door, looked inside, and, when he saw the back of the Alligator, he said, "What are those pegs that I see here? I am not a guitar-player, and I am not a violinist. I had better go to another ranch!"

The time came when the corn was to be delivered. Rabbit was at his other ranch when the Cockroach arrived. "Good-day, Uncle Rabbit!"

"Good day, Aunt Cockroach."

"I come for my corn."

"All right, only it is very early. Let us lunch first, and then we will go."

They were waiting for their lunch when they saw the Hen. The Rabbit said to the Cockroach, "Listen, Aunt Cockroach! Will not the Hen want to eat you?"

"Certainly, where shall I hide?"

The Rabbit said to her, "Madam, hide under this piece of bark here."

When the Hen arrived she said, "Good-day, Uncle Rabbit!"

"Good day, Aunt Hen!"

"I came for my corn."

"Certainly, let us first take lunch, and then we will go and shell it." The Hen sat down, and the Rabbit said to her, "Madam, would you not like to eat a cockroach?"

"Certainly," said the Hen, "where is it?"

The Rabbit showed her the cockroach under the bark, and the Rabbit said to himself, "Thus I am getting rid of my troubles."

The Rabbit and the Hen were talking when they discovered the Dog, who was coming. The Rabbit said, "Where are you going to hide, madam? For the Dog is coming, and will want to eat you. Hide under this carrying-basket." The Hen hid, and the Dog arrived.

"Good day, Uncle Rabbit!"

"Good day, Uncle Dog?"

"I came for my corn."

"Certainly! Sit down for a moment." The Dog seated himself; and the Rabbit said, "Listen, sir! Would you not like to eat a hen?"

"Where is it?"

"It is under this basket." The Dog ate the hen, and continued to talk with the Rabbit.

They were still talking when they saw the Lion; and the Rabbit asked the Dog if he was not afraid that the Lion would eat him.

The Dog said, "I am frightened. Where shall I hide?" and the Dog hid behind the house.

The Lion arrived. "Good day, Uncle Rabbit!"

"Good day, Uncle Lion!"

"I came for my corn."

The Rabbit said to him, "Sir, enter for a moment, we will go right away." The Lion entered, and the Rabbit said to him, "I'll tell you something, sir. Would you not like to eat a dog?"

"Why not? Where is it?" The Rabbit showed him where the dog was, and the Lion ate it at once.

There they were still talking when they discovered the Hunter, who was coming; and the Rabbit said, "Will he not want to kill you, sir?"

"Certainly," said the Lion. "Where shall I hide?"

"Hide on the rafter of the house. There he will not see you, sir, even if he should come. He will not do you any harm."

The Hunter arrived. "Good day, Uncle Rabbit!"

"Good day, Uncle Hunter!"

"I came for my corn."

"Certainly, Certainly," he said to him. "Come in, sir, and take a lunch first of hot cakes and fresh cheese, and then we will go to shell the corn. This is the only remaining debt that I have. Meanwhile, sir, would you not like to kill a lion?"

The Hunter said "Where is it?" The Rabbit showed him where the lion was, which the Hunter killed. The Hunter killed the lion, and during the confusion the Rabbit made his escape. When the Hunter came back to the house to look for the Rabbit, he did not find him. The Rabbit had gone away.

The Rabbit traveled on and met a Serpent, who was under a stone and could in no way get out, although she asked everyone who passed to pull her out. The Rabbit took pity on her and went to get some timbers to use to lever the stone off of her. He lifted the stone, and the Serpent was able to get out. When she was free, she wanted to eat the Rabbit.

Then he said to her, "Why do you want to do this to me? Haven't I done you a favor in taking you out from under that stone?"

The Serpent said to him, "Certainly, but don't you know that a good deed is repaid by evil deeds?"

"Allow me three witnesses before I die."

When two horses came down, the Rabbit said, "Excuse me, gentlemen! Just one word! Is it true that a good deed is repaid by an evil deed?"

"That is very true," said the Horse, "for formerly I was a good horse for my master. When he was a boy, he loved me well, and fed me well. Now I am old, and he has let me go into the fields without caring how I fare. Thus it is well said that good deeds are repaid by bad ones."

The Serpent said to him, "Now, do you see? You have only two more chances."

When two Steers passed by, the Rabbit said, "Excuse me, gentlemen! Just one word! Is it true that a good deed is repaid by evil ones?"

The Steers said, "Even if it causes sorrow, for once my master considered me a valuable animal. I served him well in my time. I was very obedient. As I served him, he loved me well. Now I am old; I am useless, and he has said that he has let me go to the field to recuperate a little, so that he can kill me."

They went on, and met a Donkey. He was standing on one side of the road, and was very sad. "Friend," said the Rabbit, "is it true that a good deed is repaid by evil ones?"

"Even if it causes sorrow," answered the Donkey, "for I gave good service to my master when he was a boy. Today, when I am old, he does not want to look at me. I just come from receiving a sound beating, which they gave me because I went to see my master."

"There is no help," said the Serpent, "you must die"

They were talking when a Rooster passed by, and he said to him, "Friend, I must die because of a good deed."

"What good deed have you done?" said the Rooster.

"I pulled the Serpent from under a stone, where she had been a long time."

The Rooster said, "How was she?"

The Serpent placed herself just in the same way as she had been under the rock, and he said, "That is the way you were placed"

The Serpent replied, "Yes."

Then he said, "If you were in this position, stay in it."

The Rabbit replied, "I owe you my life." The Rabbit and the Rooster then went their separate ways, leaving the Serpent trapped beneath the stone as before.

The Rabbit followed on his way; and as he was nearing a town, the Hunter arrived at his house, and saw the Rabbit. "There is no help this time. I'll kill you."

The Hunter put a bullet through the Rabbit. The Rabbit said, "Now I believe that a good deed is repaid by evil ones."

Source: Adapted from "Tale of the Rabbit," Franz Boas. Notes on Mexican Folklore. *Journal of American Folklore* 25 (1912): 204–260, pp. 204–210.

Brother Coyote

Coyote is a common trickster hero in the Southwest, both in Native American and Latino folklore. In many narratives, however, Coyote's greed turns him into a dupe and makes him the butt of pranks by other characters. Although Rabbit is commonly allowed to exploit Coyote's weaknesses in Latino folktales, in the present instance, Rabbit is portrayed as weak and in need of help from Lion.

It was a coyote. He was hunting for something to eat and came upon a rabbit nibbling grass. The coyote asked, "What are you eating, *Hermano Conejo* (Brother Rabbit)?"

The rabbit answered, "I am eating tender young grass."

"But, Hermanito Conejito," the coyote said, "I do not know how to eat grass. I have hunger for meat."

The poor little rabbit trembled with fear. But also he was thinking, for he had a very good head. There was an ant hill near by. The rabbit showed it to the coyote and said to him, "Here you can have some good honey that is better than meat. Keep digging and you will find it."

The coyote began scratching in the ant bed and the rabbit ran away. The large red ants swarmed out. They bit the coyote here, they bit him there; and he found no honey. He yelped with the pain. "Ay! ay! ay!" He rolled over and over to rid himself of the ants, and the more he suffered the angrier he became with the rabbit for fooling him.

So he ran after Hermano Conejo, and when he caught up with him he said, "Now, you tricky rabbit, I'm going to eat you."

"No, do not eat me, Hermano Coyote," said the rabbit, and quickly he began knocking ripe prickly pears from a nopal [cactus]. "Eat these pears instead; they are very sweet this year and much more succulent than rabbit meat."

While the greedy coyote stopped to taste the fruit the rabbit got away. He ran far, but at last he had to stop at a water hole because he was tired and had much thirst. He was still drinking when a mountain lion, a panther, came.

"Don't waste time drinking water, little brother rabbit," the lion warned him, "a coyote is coming close behind me. Run quickly before he gets here and eats you up. Leave the coyote to me; I'll attend to him. Hurry!"

So the little rabbit ran on, and in this way he escaped. When the coyote reached the water hole, the lion alone was there to greet him.

"Good morning, Hermano Coyote, where are you going so fast?"

"I am chasing a rabbit because he would not give me meat."

"Wait a little while," said the lion, "and I shall get you all the meat you wish. What kind of meat do you know how to eat?"

The coyote answered, "I know how to eat field mice and rabbits and goats and sheep. I know how to eat little calves and chickens and all such things."

"But I do not kill that kind of meat," said the lion. "I like young mules and horses. In all the world there is no meat as tasty as that of a colt."

"Just get me any kind of meat," said the coyote. "For the love of God, hurry, Hermano Lion, for I am almost dead of hunger."

"All right," said the lion, "I shall climb up this tree. You hide below and make yourself ready. I see a cloud of dust."

"Just what is it?

"A herd of mares and colts coming to water. Keep quiet; do not move, Hermano Coyote."

The lion and the coyote kept very still. The mares and their herd of colts stopped to drink. A yearling colt came close, and the lion sprang from the tree to its back. The surprised colt bucked and pitched.

"Hold on, Hermano Lion," cried the coyote, full of delight. "*No te flojes, campadre!* Hang on, pardner espuelas! Scrape him with the spurs! Ride him, cowboy!"

The lion rode the colt well, just like a vaquero [cowboy], and in no time had it by the throat and killed it. "Here is your meat, Hermano Coyote," he said, "and now you see how one kills a colt."

"Yes, but you have spurs to hold on with," said the coyote.

"And you, also, have spurs," said the lion. "Have you not nails on your toes as well as I? Now I have taught you how to get meat, I shall leave, Hermano Coyote."

The lion left, and the coyote ate until he could eat no more. But another day came when he had hunger. So he said to himself, I see a cloud of dust in the distance. It must be the herd. Perhaps there may be another fat colt in the bunch, and I can kill it as Hermano Lion showed me."

The herd drew closer, and, sure enough, there was a young mule that was fine and fat. While it was drinking at the water hole, the coyote sprang upon its back. But Hermano Coyote was not a vaquero; he did not know how to ride, and his spurs were no good. The mule bucked but once and off Hermano Coyote rolled to the rocky ground. The mule kicked him here, the mule kicked him there; he kicked him on the nose; he kicked him all over. "Ay! ay!" Hermano Coyote yelped and swore, limping away as fast as he could. Soon he met the lion.

"What's the matter with you, Hermano Coyote?" the lion asked, trying not to laugh. "You look rather ill."

The coyote was very angry. "What's the matter with me? Just look and you will see how bruised and near death I am from doing as you told me."

"Oh, but you do not know how to get on in the world." The lion laughed and laughed. "You will die of hunger yet. But here are many deer and antelope. See if you can get one of them. They do not buck like mules and horses. Look how they are passing. Put on your spurs well because these animals will run away with you if you are not careful."

"But how can I catch one?" asked the coyote. "Please, Hermano Lion, help me; show me how it is done."

"Which one do you want?"

"I want that young doe."

"Very well then, Hermano Coyote. I'll get in this tree and you start the bunch running this way. Then you come and help me here."

"Good," said the coyote. "Now I shall get my fill."

He cut out the doe he wanted and drove her directly under the tree where the lion waited. Hermano Lion sprang upon the doe's back; Hermano Coyote helped, and together they killed her. The lion ate what he wanted first, as lions always do, and left all the rest for the greedy coyote.

Once more a day came when the coyote had great hunger, and this time he was all alone. He wished to kill another deer and he was sure he knew how it was done. Although coyotes do not climb well, he managed to get into a tree as the lion had taught him. There he waited and waited for a deer to come by. At last when he was almost dying from hunger, a foolish deer stopped to graze beneath the tree. The coyote leaped upon its back. But it was not a young doe. It was a very strong, old buck.

The coyote dug his spurs into the buck's flanks and tried to stop him, but the buck only ran faster and faster. As the coyote could not ride like a cowboy and as his spurs were too small, he soon rolled off the buck's back and over a bank into a deep hole in the river. The banks of the river were so slick and steep Hermano Coyote could not get out.

Because he was greedy and not content with eating the food God wished him to eat, he was drowned.

Source: Adapted from "Br'er Coyote," Sarah S. McKellar. *Puro Mexicano,* J. Frank Dobie, ed. *Publications of the Texas Folklore Society,* no. 12 (Austin: Texas Folk-Lore Society, 1935), pp. 101–106.

Sister Fox and Brother Coyote

"Sister Fox and Brother Coyote" displays the blending of European and Native American features typical of Latino folktales in the Southwest. Coyote, who appears in "Brother Coyote" and "Tale of the Rabbit," as well as in the following story, is a popular character throughout the folklore of Western and Southwestern Native America. Fox, while not entirely absent from Native American narratives, is more common in European trickster tales. While the following folktale shares many episodes with "Brother Coyote" and "Tales of Rabbit," casting Fox as trickster and Coyote as dupe gives it a unique twist.

For weeks *'Mana Zorra* [Hermana, Sister] Fox had been stealing a chicken each night from a ranch not far from her abode when one night she found a small man standing near the opening she had made in the wire of the chicken house. The man was only a figure of wax put there by the *caporal* [ranch foreman] to frighten the thief. 'Mana Zorra, unaware of this, was afraid, but, being very hungry, she decided to speak to the little man and ask permission to borrow a chicken.

"*Buenas noches* [good evening]," said 'Mana Zorra.

There was no answer.

"He is either too proud to speak or doesn't hear," said the fox to herself. "If he isn't *mal criado* (ill-bred), then he didn't hear. I will speak to him again."

Going nearer the wax man, she said, "*Buenas noches, señor.*"

The little man made no response whatsoever, and the fox, after sizing him up from feet to head, decided that she had been insulted.

"Ay, the things I'm going to tell this *hombrecito* [little man]," said she. "He shall speak to me this time or I will slap his face."

She walked up to the figure and shouted at the top of her voice, "Step aside, please, and let me pass."

The wax man stubbornly stood his ground and refused to speak.

"Now you shall see how I make you move to one side," said 'Mana Zorra. She struck the little man in the face and much to her surprise her foot was caught and held fast.

"Let me go!" shouted 'Mana Zorra, "or I shall hit you again."

The wax man refused to let go and 'Mana Zorra hit him full in the face with a hard right swing. The result was that this foot too, like the other, was caught and held.

"Listen," grumbled 'Mana Zorra. "Listen, *amigo,* either you let me go or I shall give you a kicking you will never forget."

The wax man was not impressed by the threat and refused to let go. 'Mana Zorra made good her word as to the kicking, but the little man didn't seem to mind at all and added insult to injury by holding her hind feet too.

"I'll bite," she threatened; "I'll bite." And quickly she bit the neck of the wax figure only to find herself caught not only by four feet but by her mouth as well.

"You think you have me," she scolded. "All right, how do you like this for a belly buster?" She pushed him so hard with her stomach that both of them fell rolling to the ground. Just then who should appear on the scene but *'Mano* [Hermano, Brother] Coyote? "What are you doing there, 'Mana Zorra?" he asked.

"No, nothing," she answered. "This Christian and I have come to blows over a chicken. I have a contract with the ranchero which provides me a hen a night, but this little fellow can't read and has made up his mind to inter-fere. Hold him for me, 'Mano Coyote, and I will get a hen for both of us."

The coyote, a gullible fellow, caught the wax man in a clinch and held him while the fox pulled loose, and continued to hold tight until she stole a hen and escaped into the chaparral. Then, much to his chagrin, he found that he had been tricked, and as a result would likely lose his life.

Dawn found 'Mano Coyote struggling with the wax man, and he was there and still fighting when the caporal arrived.

"Ah, my little friend," said the caporal. "This is what I have been wanting to find out for a long time. So it is you, *Señor Coyote?* And I had always thought you my friend. If you wanted a hen to eat, why didn't you come to me like a gentleman and ask for her? However, though greatly disappointed in you, I will give you another chance."

The caporal freed the coyote from the wax man and placed him in a little room with one broken window. "Don't jump through this window till I call you," said the ranch foreman to the coyote. "My dogs will catch and kill you. Wait until I tie them up and get us a snack to eat. Then when I call, jump through the window and come to the kitchen."

The caporal heated water and poured it into a large pot that he had placed beneath the window. Then he called, "Come out, Señor Coyote; breakfast is ready."

The coyote jumped through the window and fell into the pot of boiling water. It was surely a miracle that saved his life, but the scalding water took the hair from his body and several toe nails from his feet.

"Ay, ay," said 'Mano Coyote, as he crept with flinching feet and sore hide through the thicket. " 'Mana Zorra will pay for this. If I ever see her again I will kill her and eat her up."

Thus went 'Mano Coyote through the brush whining and swearing revenge until he reached a *laguna* [lake]. There, before him, lay the fox gazing at something in the water.

"Now 1 have you," cried the coyote. "Now you are to pay for your smart trick."

"Don't kill me, 'Mano Coyotito," pleaded the fox. "Look! I was placed here to watch this cheese."

"What cheese?" asked the coyote.

The moon was full and the reflection lay at the bottom of the laguna.

"There," said the fox, pointing at the reflection. "If you will watch it for me I will get us a chicken. However, be on guard lest the cheese slip beneath the bank."

"I'll watch it for you," said the coyote, "but don't be long. I'm dying for a chicken to eat."

'Mano Coyote had waited and watched several hours when he discovered the cheese slipping beneath the western bank of the laguna.

"Hey, Señor Cheese, don't go away," he called. "If you run away, I'll catch you and eat you up."

While 'Mano Coyote talked, the cheese continued to slip away. The coyote, fearing it would escape, sprang into the laguna and was soaked and chilled to the marrow before he reached the bank again.

" 'Mana Zorra will pay for this," he howled. "Wherever I find her I shall kill her and eat her up."

The coyote had hunted the fox several days when at last he found her lying on her back in a small cave beneath a cropping of boulders. She was sound asleep.

"A' 'Mana Zorrita," hissed the coyote, "now I shall eat you up."

"Don't eat me, 'Mano *Coyotito*," begged the fox. "Look! When I went to get a hen, the caporal asked me to lie here and hold the world on my feet to keep it from falling down. He has gone to get more help and will be back soon to fix it. *Ay de mí* [exclamation], 'Mano Coyote, I'm hungry. I know where there is a hen, but she will likely be gone when the caporal returns. Ay de mí, 'Mano Coyote, I'm hungry."

"I'm hungry, too," said the coyote. "Look, 'Mana Zorra, move over to one side. I'll hold the world on my feet if you will hurry and fetch us a hen."

"Good," said the fox, "but take care that the world doesn't fall and come to an end."

"I'll hold it," said the coyote lying on his back and pushing up with the strength of all four of his feet. "However, hurry, I'm hungry"

The fox escaped, and the coyote remained beneath the rock for several hours until he was almost paralyzed by the increasing weight of the world.

At last, being unable longer to stand the pain of his cramped position, he said, "If it is going to fall, then let it fall. I'm quitting this job."

He sprang from beneath the ledge and ran into the clearing. The rock didn't fall and the world showed no signs of coming to an end.

"Ay, ay," said he, " 'Mana Zorra shall pay for this. If I ever catch her I shall kill her and eat her up."

At last the fox was found beneath a large bush near a *gicotera* [a rat's nest at the roots of a bush where hornets sometimes nest].

"A', 'Mana Zorra," he cried, "you have played your last trick, for now I'm going to eat you up."

"Don't eat me, 'Mano Coyotito," begged the fox. "Look! I was on my way to get the chicken when a school teacher offered me pay to watch a class of boys."

"Where are the boys?" asked the coyote.

"There, before us; it is their schoolroom," the fox said as she pointed to the hornet's nest.

"Where is the money?" asked the coyote further.

"In my pocket," said the fox, as she rattled some pieces of porcelain.

"That's good," said the coyote. "What are you going to do with it?"

"I'm going to buy you a pair of trousers and a skirt for myself."

"Your idea is good," observed the coyote. "However, you must leave some money with which to purchase food."

"Certainly," said the fox. "I shall buy us a chicken a piece. But why did you mention food, 'Mano Coyote? *Ay, ay de mí,* I'm dying of hunger."

"I'm hungry, too," said the coyote.

"Look!" said the fox. "Watch these boys for me and I'll fetch the hen right away."

"*Cómo no* [Why not]?" said the coyote; "only hurry, 'Mana Zorra."

The fox saved her hide again and the coyote was left with the devil to pay, for the schoolroom was a hornets' nest and the boys were not pupils but a lively lot of hornets.

The coyote sat listening to the hum of pupils reading their lessons when he noticed that the sound had ceased. "They are loafing on me," he said. "I'll shake them up a bit."

He shook them up and this would have been his last adventure had he not found a laguna into which to dive and escape the swarm of hornets.

"Ay, ay," wailed the coyote. " 'Mana Zorra shall pay for this. Wherever it is that I find her I shall eat her up, hide and hair."

At last 'Mana Zorra was found in a *carrizal*—a reed swamp.

'Mano Coyote had not forgotten the hornets' sting, the moon cheese, the world trick, and the wax man. "Now there shall be no more foolishness," said he. " 'Mana Zorra must die."

"Don't eat me," pleaded the fox. "Don't eat me, 'Mano Coyotito. Look! I was on my way to get the hens when I met a bridegroom. He invited me to be godmother at his wedding. I felt it would look bad to refuse, and now that you are here you and I shall be *pardrino* [godfather] and *madrina* [godmother]. You know how it is at these weddings. There is always plenty to eat and drink, and when it comes to chicken, there is none better in the world than that served at a wedding feast. Ay, ay, I'm hungry, 'Mano Coyotito."

Said the coyote; "I'm hungry, too. But where is the wedding party?"

"They are to pass at any time now," said the fox. "You stay here, and I'll see if they are coming. If you hear popping and cracking you will know it is the fireworks shot by the friends of the couple. I shall be back soon."

'Mana Zorra slipped around the cane brake and set fire to it in first one place and then another. 'Mano Coyote heard the popping and cracking and began to dance with joy.

"*Taco Talaco*," said he, "here they come. *Taco Talaco, ay, Taco Talaco,* what a hot time there will be."

He discovered his mistake too late. The fire had trapped him completely, and so ended the career of 'Mano Coyote the dupe, shouting "*Taco Talaco*" and dancing at his own funeral.

Source: "Sister Fox and Brother Coyote" from "A Packload of Mexican Tales," Riley Aiken. *Puro Mexicano,* J. Frank Dobie, ed. *Publications of the Texas Folklore Society,* no. 12 (Austin: Texas Folk-Lore Society, 1935), pp. 13–19.

Pedro de Urdemalas

Pedro de Urdemalas is the classic human trickster hero of the Latino Southwest. Like any good con man, he exploits the vices and foolishness of others to achieve his own ends. Unlike Coyote in "Tale of the Rabbit" and "Brother Coyote," he is clever enough to escape the punishment his swindles have earned for him.

Pedro de Urdemalas lives by his wits. In a way he is a liar, but he does not lie for the glory of lying. His lies are a means to an end, and the most desirable end to him is to skin the fellow who is out to get the other man's hide. However, he often tricks the innocently gullible. Also, being a man of chance, he is a plaything of fate; one day he is rich and the next poor.

Once when considerably the worse for his manner of living and while wandering along a highway tired, hungry, and without money, he came to a hog ranch. It was the first of its kind he had ever seen and, despite his low spirits, he was greatly amused by the great array of swine tails.

"There are many tails," said he, "wherever there is a tail there is a hog. This gives me an idea, and if it works I shall have money to spend."

He took his knife and cut the tails from the hogs and continued on his way until he came to a swamp. There he busied himself sticking the hog-end of the tail stumps in the mud. Then, after tramping around and digging up the earth about each, he sat beneath a willow and began to weep.

Presently a man rode up horseback. "Why are you weeping?" he asked.

Pedro wept louder than ever and said, "Why shouldn't I weep? I have lost a fortune in this bog hole. Those tails you see are all that is left to show for hogs that were."

"Poor fellow," said the stranger, "weep no more. I shall buy your herd and have my servants come and dig them out of this mud. How much do you want for them?"

"Señor," said Pedro de Urdemalas, "it is not my wish to sell them, for life is wrapped up in my hogs, but you see how hopeless things are. Rather than lose them, I will sell them to you for one thousand dollars."

The trade was made. Pedro went away weeping until he was out of sight and then took to his heels.

The stranger brought his servants, and he was not long finding out how well he had been swindled. Frantic, he directed a search for Pedro but all to no avail. He gave up the hunt and did the only thing left for him to do, and that was to swear revenge in case he should ever again meet Pedro de Urdemalas.

Well, sir, true to form, there came a day when again Pedro was broke and hungry. Immediately he began devising a new lie with which to snare some sucker. "I need twenty cents worth of frijoles, a pot, an underground furnace, and a little time," said he to himself.

He bought beans and pot, dug a furnace, and, after having burned some wood to coals, he put the pot over them and hid all traces of the fire. Presently the pot began to boil, and Pedro, with a long thorn, speared those frijoles that boiled to the top and ate them. He was amusing himself in this manner when a traveler approached.

"*Buenas tardes, buen amigo* (good day, good friend)," he said. "What are you doing?"

"No, nothing," said Pedro de Urdemalas, "just waiting for those who are to arise and observing those who go."

"Pardon," said the traveler, pointing at the pot, "what makes that thing boil?"

"Nothing; it is a magic pot," Pedro informed him. "In the preparation of my meals I never have to bother with fire. So soon as the food is in it and it is placed on the ground it begins to boil."

Now, the stranger was a traveling man and figured that he needed just such a pot. "How much do you want for it?" he asked.

"I don't care to sell it," said Pedro.

"I will give you a thousand dollars," bartered the traveler.

"See here, amigo," said Pedro de Urdemalas, "I am badly in need of money; otherwise I would not think of disposing of such a rare pot. It is a bargain, but we will have to take care lest it discover the change in masters and refuse to boil. Sit down very quietly and give me the money. Don't speak or move until I am out of hearing."

It was with the utmost caution that the trade was made. The stranger, almost afraid to breathe, sat by the boiling pot and Pedro tiptoed away. After an hour of patient watching the new owner of the magic vessel noticed that the beans and water were not boiling. He picked up the pot and immediately realized that he had been skinned. At first he swore revenge, but after a second thought he was so humiliated by his gullibility that he was glad to forget about it.

It was late in the afternoon when Pedro de Urdemalas decided it would be safe to rest his weary legs. Tired out by the haste with which he left his last victim, he sat beneath a mesquite not far from the road and wondered how he might add another thousand dollars to his ill-gotten gain. Presently, he began by boring holes in the coin he carried, and, when this was done, he hung it to the branches of the tree in such a manner that it appeared to have grown there. The following morning two wagon masters on their way up the road were amazed by what they saw. They went to the mesquite and were at the point of plucking the rare fruit when Pedro saw them.

"*Eit, eit!*" he shouted. "Leave my tree alone."

They asked the name of the tree.

"This is the only one in existence," said Pedro de Urdemalas. "It bears twice a year and it is time to gather this season's crop."

"How much do you want for this plant?" they asked.

"Don't insult me," said Pedro. "Why should I want to sell a tree like this? It would be foolish."

"We can pay your price," they insisted. "Besides, it isn't our intention to leave here before you agree to sell."

"Oh, well," said Pedro, "give me a thousand dollars and the present crop and the bargain is closed."

They agreed. Pedro gathered the coin from the tree, collected the purchase money, and left for parts unknown.

The wagon masters built homes near the mesquite, pruned it, watered it, and did all in their power to aid in a rich crop of coin the following season. It being only a mesquite, their reward was mesquite beans. These poor fools, like the others, had been beaten, but were thankful to have come off no worse.

Pedro, in the meantime, was, as an old song says, always traveling. One day, however, much to his surprise and great concern, he met a giant.

"Ay, Chihuahua!" said he, "this is an ugly business. How am I to manage now?"

Quickly, before the giant had seen him he took a sandal from his foot and threw it into the air.

"What do you say?" said the giant when he saw Pedro. "If you feel strong, let's see if you can whip me."

Just then the sandal fell.

"What's this?" asked the giant.

Then Pedro de Urdemalas explained that three days previous he had thrown a man into the air and this sandal was the first he had seen of him since.

The giant was frightened and figured that if that were the case it might be advisable to go easy with Pedro, However, gathering new courage, he said, "I'll bet you my life against yours you can't beat me at three stunts I know."

"What do you mean?" asked Pedro.

"First," said the giant, "let's see you ram your arm through the heart of this tree."

Pedro asked that he be given a day to prepare for the feat, and the giant agreed to the request and went away.

Pedro de Urdemalas thought for a long time. Then carefully he removed the bark from a large tree; after hollowing out a place in the trunk the size of his fist and the length of his arm, he placed its bark back again.

The next day the giant returned and asked if Pedro were ready to attempt the first feat. Upon being assured that he was, the giant said, "Choose your tree."

"I'll take this one," said Pedro, "and, since I accepted the challenge, I'll hit first."

He walked to the tree and with an easy jab sent his fist an arm's length into the trunk. The giant admitted he was beaten and chose not to hit.

"The second feat," said he, "is to see who can throw a stone the farther."

Having been granted a day for preparation and the giant having gone away, Pedro de Urdemalas caught a quail, and on the following morning hid it beneath his blouse.

The giant returned, chose to throw first, and sent a stone a quarter of a league before it came to earth.

"Stand away," said Pedro. "I must wind up." And while the giant was not looking, Pedro pretended to throw and turned the quail loose. "There it goes," said he. The bird passed out of sight while still rising into the air.

The giant admitted that Pedro's stone had gone the farther.

Tomorrow we will wrestle, he said.

Pedro de Urdemalas spent the night tearing up the soil and the breaking down the chaparral. He tore his clothes and scratched his hands.

The next morning when the giant asked the meaning of the strange disorder Pedro replied, "No, nothing; I've been fighting a man larger than you."

"Where is he?" asked the giant.

"I threw him into the air and he hasn't come down yet," said Pedro.

"Pedro," said the giant, "I'm glad to admit you are the better man. However, before you take my life come be my guest tonight in my home."

In the guest's room immediately above the bed there hung by a trigger a large iron bar released by a rope back of the door. After supper Pedro de Urdemalas was shown to bed. But not for nothing had Pedro lived by his wits, and before long he discovered the trap. He arranged the covers so as to suggest a body beneath them and hid behind the door.

At midnight the giant quietly entered the room and crept to the bedside to see just how the sleeper lay. When he leaned over the bed, Pedro released the iron bar and the giant was killed.

Pedro left this place. Three days later, while walking along the road, he came face to face with the man who had bought the swine tails.

"Now you are going to pay," said the man, catching Pedro by the arm. "You have had a lot of fun during your life, but now that is all over."

"It is all very true," said Pedro. "Dispose of me whenever you please."

Pedro de Urdemalas was taken to the man's ranch and there was placed in a large barrel. The lid was fastened on the barrel, and one little hole was bored in the side.

"We will eat dinner," said the man to the servants, "and then we will take him to the river and drown him."

Pedro remained quiet until they were out of hearing and then began rocking the barrel. This had been left near a slope, and when at last it turned over it began rolling away from the house and came to a halt in a meadow near a herd of sheep.

"Buen amigo, buen amigo!" called Pedro.

A herder came to the barrel and asked, "What's the matter?"

"Nothing at all except that they are trying to compel me to marry the king's only daughter," said Pedro. "If you care to, you may take my place."

"Is this true?" asked the herder.

"Yes," said Pedro, "it's true; only get me out of here and you get in."

The change was made and the barrel was rolled back to the top of the slope and placed where the man and his servants had left it. Then Pedro gathered the sheep and drove them away.

In due time the barrel and contents were thrown into the river, and, as it sank from sight, there came the gurgling sound, "gori-gori-gori!"

Some days later the man and his servants were hunting. "Isn't that the man we drowned?" said one of them, pointing to a herder some distance away.

"I'll swear it is," said the man.

They approached and spoke to Pedro de Urdemalas. "I thought you were drowned," said the man.

"Didn't you hear the gori-gori-gori when the barrel sank?" asked Pedro. "Well, each gori was a sheep. Once the barrel was on the bottom of the river, the underwater people opened it and let me go."

"What shall we do with him, boys?" said the man.

"He's had enough," said the servants. "Let him go."

Pedro Urdemalas sold his sheep and entered the king's service. The ruler was a great tease and made life miserable for his servants. However, Pedro turned the trick on him so often the king was offended.

"Take this rascal and hang him," said he.

"Grant me a last request," pleaded Pedro.

"Very well," said the king.

"Let me choose the tree upon which I'm to be hanged."

"Granted," said the king. "Soldiers, go hang him and never let me see his face or hear of him again."

Pedro de Urdemalas chose to be hanged to a sunflower plant. The soldiers were perplexed. They had heard the last wish granted and also they were afraid to bring the matter again to the king's attention. Consequently, they released Pedro de Urdemalas on condition that he never show his face again.

Source: Adapted from "Pedro de Urdemalas," A Packload of Mexican Tales, Riley Aiken. *Puro Mexicano,* J. Frank Dobie, ed. (Dallas: Southern Methodist University Press, 1935), pp. 48–54.

Pablo Apodaca and the Bear

The following local New Mexico legend in many ways resembles fictional tales of the "dragon-slayer" type. Pablo is a representative of the people, a hero who displays the characteristics necessary for life in his chosen environment—strength, bravery, and resourcefulness— in their fullest development. He heroically kills a "monster" with his bare hands, thus making the world safer for his neighbors. He also reveals a tragic flaw, however, an overconfidence in his own abilities. This flaw leads him into a foolhardy act that almost costs him his life.

Pablo Apodaca was the strongest man in New Mexico in his day. That was thirty years ago, but still, in the quaint little Mexican towns, if you join the lazy groups squatted against the brown adobe walls, smoking their corn-husk cigarettes, and ask the old men who is the strongest wrestler thereabout, they will say, "Who knows? Juan can knock down a horse with his fist, and Domingo can carry the heaviest cross of the Penitentes all day, but you ought to have known Pablo Apodaca! He was the strongest man that ever was. May God give his soul rest!"

If Pablo could have been seen in Boston or New York, the whole police force of the city hardly would have sufficed to keep a mob of astonished boys from following in his wake whenever he went upon the street, for they never saw such a queer sight as he would have presented.

A short, heavy man, whose long, black hair and bushy beard hid his great neck so that his head seemed grown fast to his shoulders; a chest like a barrel, and legs so bowed that his friends used to say that he could not hold his baby in his lap without letting it fall through; a big Mexican blanket falling nearly to his knees on all sides, and with his head stuck through a hole in the middle of it; flapping pantaloons of rough cloth, and feet covered with clumsy teguas, he certainly was a queer object. And when he thrust out his arms from under the blanket, and rolled up his sleeves as he was rather fond of doing the full, blue veins stood out like knotted whipcords over great gnarls and lumps of muscle that Atlas himself might have envied.

Pablo lived in Cebolleta, one of the tiniest towns in New Mexico; but small as it is, none has a more heroic history. Pablo's father was one of the thirty Mexican men who came from the Rio Grande with their families in

the year 1800, and founded their little town, 75 miles west of any other settlement, and in the very midst of the murderous Navajos. They built a strong
stone wall, ten feet high, all around the few houses, and had but one gate
thereto a clumsy but lasting affair of thick planks hewn from the trunk of
an enormous pine. Several times the hamlet was besieged by Indians, but
the brave people, behind their stout ramparts, held the savages at bay.

It required brave people to hold such a place. For more than half a century
the little town rarely knew a month of peace, and in 1850 the very bravest
and best of its soldiers were massacred in their sleep at San Miguel by the
Apaches; but the survivors remained at their post, and Cebolleta still dreams
away on the rugged flank of Mt. San Mateo, the ruins of its old wall crum-
bling around it.

It was among such scenes of danger that Pablo grew up, along with a little
company of other self-reliant young Mexicans. It would have been hard to
tell who was bravest, but as to strength there was no question. Pablo could
lift more and carry more than any other man in the town, and when it came
to wrestling, no one cared to try his skill twice. No matter how expert they
were, when once that iron clutch fastened upon them, they were powerless
as children; and Pablo was as quick as he was strong. Then he began to
travel to the feasts with which the various hamlets celebrated the days of
their patron saints, and in the wrestling matches, which were part of the
sport, Pablo made all comers bite the dust. So by the time he was a mature
man, his name was a proverb throughout the Province of New Mexico
which had not yet become a territory of the United States.

All this exercise, with the simple food he ate and the rugged outdoor life
he led, kept his knotted muscles growing larger and harder. When he was
30 years of age, he used to catch a five-year-old steer by the horns, and hold
the great brute so firmly that it seemed as if lashed to some mighty oak.

Strength is a quality that always commands admiration, and, rightly used,
ought also to command respect; but Pablo came to have too much strength for
his own good. That is hardly a fair way to put it, either, for it was not the
strength which was at fault, but rather Pablo's own ignorance how to use it
wisely. From never meeting an opponent that he could not conquer, he came
to believe that nothing could stand against him; and I have no doubt that he
would cheerfully have undertaken a wrestle with a locomotive, if they had had
such strange monsters in New Mexico then in place of the clumsy old ox carts.

In his young manhood Pablo married a pretty Mexican girl, after her
father had kept him at work in dangerous expeditions for a whole year to
see if he was as industrious as he was strong. They lived together happily.
Pablo tended his little flock of sheep, while Juanita carded the wool, wove
homely but durable blankets, carpets and clothing, and attended to her
other household duties.

In one of his campaigns Pablo had captured a strong Navajo girl, and
brought her home as a present for his prospective bride as the custom of New

Mexico then required all young men to do before they could expect to marry.
When Pablo was away fighting the Indians which was a great deal of the time
Juanita and the Navajo girl, who had grown to be very fond of each other, took
all the care of things at home. A great many white men would turn pale at the
thought of doing what those two brave young women did for life
on the Southwestern frontier in those days was full alike of hardship and of
danger.

As the years went by the little household grew. If you could have stepped
into the small plaza, or square, on which all the houses of Cebolleta faced,
you might have seen Pablo sitting in his doorway mending his teguas with
an awl and some threads of deer-sinew. The soles were of rawhide, the
uppers of sheepskin with the wool inside. Near him Juanita was very sure
to be, perhaps twisting her wool for weaving, or scrubbing blue corn into a
pulp on the lava metate [grinding stone]. And around the door played a trio
of strong, healthy boys, with whom Pablo—good-natured as such strong
men generally are—sometimes took a rough romp.

One time when the Navajos were quiet, Pablo took it into his head to
stroll over the mountain to the newer village of San Mateo, and to take his
oldest boy with him. Few American boys of twelve years would have
enjoyed tramping twenty-two miles over that fearfully rough and steep footpath, but Pablito, besides being delighted with the rare chance to go
anywhere with the father of whom he was so proud, was a sturdy boy, and
not easily tired. So while Pablo was carefully loading his ponderous *esco-
peta,* as the Mexican flint-lock musket was called, Pablito poked his head
through the gay red blanket his mother had woven for him, and filled a
buckskin pouch with pounded dry meat and a sweet flour made from
popcorn. The meat was all ready to be eaten; and by mixing the pinole with
water they would have a sort of sweet mush, itself nutritious enough to
support life for a long time.

It was a cool, fresh day in May. May days in Cebolleta, over 7,000 feet
above the sea level, are always cool and Pablo and Pablito were in great
spirits as they climbed the steep, winding path up the mesa or tableland.
Pablo had never been so strong as he was that day, and he knew it. The deep
satisfaction of his lungs, the conscious swelling of his muscles, all told him.
He felt as if he would like to pluck one of those gnarled cedars up by the
roots and hurl it far down the mountain.

Up, up they climbed. The cedars gave place to noble pines. Though the
sun was at its height, the air was growing cooler; and upon the giant peak
at their right they could see the vast white drifts which would lie there until
the earlier heat of July. The path was fearfully rugged. It wound around
enormous boulders, dived into dark ravines, and struggled up precipitous
banks.

A needle-pointed dagger of the soap-root went through Pablito's clumsy
tegua and deep into his foot; but his herculean father took him upon his

back as if he had been a feather, and strode on. They were passing the brink of a great bluff, nearly three hundred feet high and very precipitous, when a turn in the narrow path brought them face to face with a young grizzly bear cub. Pablo dropped Pablito gently from his back, and gave him the ponderous musket, which he could hardly hold up.

"Hold, my boy," said Pablo, "and I will tie that cub so that we may get him when we come back. He is young enough to tame."

Pulling two strong buckskin thongs from his *bolsa* [bag], he rushed upon the cub, threw it, and began to knot its four clumsy paws together. The cub scratched and snapped like a little fiend, but Pablo's gigantic strength enabled him to draw up the knots, which he wet with his mouth, that they might tighten as they dried.

But he had not tied the young grizzly's mouth, and from those little long jaws there issued a steady shriek. It is one of the strangest sounds in nature, the yelling of an enraged bear cub a grotesque mixture of pig-squeal, hoarse steam whistle, sputter, and bark.

Other ears heard it than Pablo's and Pablito's. Suddenly the boy screamed, "La osa [the bear]! La osa!"

There was a great scuffling in the gravel around the point and a wild rush. Before Pablo could stand straight, the huge old mother-bear had dealt him a cuff on the back of the neck that sent him spinning. He was up again like a cat, dazed but undismayed, and in a flash the shaggy monster was again upon him, but now face to face.

There was no time to run; and Pablo could not get his musket, so, with the instinct of the practiced wrestler, he ducked and caught a grip in the bear's rough fur. He hugged her in a grip that might have killed an ordinary man himself so close that the bear could not strike him and kept his head well down out of reach of the creature's great jaws.

I fancy the bear was surprised by this unusual state of affairs, but she kept her thoughts to herself. Throwing her huge, short "arms" around Pablo, she returned his hug with interest. He had grappled the strongest men scores of times, but never had he felt such a pressure as that. It seemed to be crushing his very life out. But Pablo's heart was as strong as his body, and he never thought of giving up. He put forth all his gigantic strength, till the blue veins upon his forehead stood out like strong cords. He swayed his huge foe from side to side as if her eight hundred pounds had been but a man's weight. He tried to trip her, and did once fling her upon her side.

But the odds of weight and they were fearful odds were against him, and he found his breath failing under his own enormous efforts and that superhuman hug. And still he struggled. In that blind, savage melée they tore up the rocky path, and broke off a young pine, and on a sudden, overstepping the narrow battlefield, man and bear went rolling down the precipitous bluff, locked in deadly embrace.

Pablito had watched the fight with breathless interest, and with firm faith in the triumph of his father. But now he was horror stricken; and forgetting his pierced foot, he dashed down the hill, still hugging the musket with both arms, tumbling headlong, cutting himself on the sharp rocks, but bouncing up again like a rubber ball, and dashing on.

Pablo and the bear had stopped rolling. The three hundred feet of tumble had cut Pablo's head fearfully, and half stunned him. His great strength was almost gone, and he could no longer strain himself to such close quarters as to escape the bear's jaws. He was lying on his back, feebly fighting the animal off with his right arm. The left had been crushed by the bear's jaws, and lay twisted beside him. Above him was the enraged animal, her jaws dripping blood, and her wicked little eyes snapping like firebrands.

"My boy!" Pablo called, in a faint, ghostly voice the boy hardly knew, "Shoot! Shoot!"

"But I am afraid of shooting you! I don't know how!" shrieked Pablito, sobbing. The light weapons of today were unknown then, and Pablito had never fired a gun in his life.

"Don't mind me. Put the muzzle to her side and fire," came Pablo's answer, so faintly it could just be heard. With a mighty effort of the will he struck the bear a blow on the nose that made her snort with pain to distract her attention from the boy.

Pablito was trembling and sobbing, but he was of the stuff that men are made. He pulled back the heavy hammer, lifted the muzzle painfully, held it forward till it touched the shaggy fur, and pulled the trigger.

The bear lurched heavily forward, bit a great mouthful out of the earth, struggled a few minutes, and then lay motionless. The ounce ball had passed through her heart, and also through Pablo's right thigh.

Pablito ran madly down the long mountain side for help, and soon a score of rough men hastened to the spot, and carried Pablo home on a rude litter of boughs. For weeks the herb-wise old women who helped Juanita to care for him were often in doubt whether that faint pulse had not stopped. And then his iron constitution asserted itself. The pulse grew stronger, the yawning cavities in face and chest began to close, and at last Pablo Apodaca was a well man.

But when, for the first time, he hobbled outside his own door, the neighboring children fled in terror at the sight of the scarred, disfigured face that had been so strong and ruddy. His nose was gone; his cheeks and chin and forehead were robbed of their covering.

Pablo never wrestled again, though he lived for several years longer. But his fame still lasts. And if you were to happen into Cebolleta of a summer's evening you might see Pablito now grown to manhood telling a black-eyed boy "about your grandfather, and the time I killed my first bear."

Source: C. F. Lummis, *A New Mexico David and Other Stories and Sketches of the Southwest* (New York: Charles Scribner's Sons, 1891), pp. 68–78.

SOCIETY AND CONFLICT

Manuel Jesus Vasques: A Life on the Southwest Frontier

The image of the great bison (buffalo) herds on the Plains is one of the icons of American history. The character of the hide hunters and their Sharps rifles has transcended life into pop culture via media from the "dime novel" to the Hollywood feature film. Contemporary images, however, rarely reflect the historical reality of this life. Another side of the story is revealed through the life of Manuel Jesus Vasques who—hunting, not with a Sharps rifle, but with a lance from horseback—made his patron a wealthy man. Vasques was cheated of his inheritance, while "never holding a single penny in his hand." His oral biography presents a reality of the Latino buffalo hunter and horse trader unlike any accounts captured in the contemporary mass media.

Don Manuel Jesus Vasques was born in the settlement of Chamisal, Taos County, New Mexico on the 31st day of January of the year 1856. He himself does not know how he came to live at the home of Don Juan Policarpio Romero of the village of Penasco but at the age of eight he was herdboy for a flock of goats belonging to Don Juan Policarpio Romero and continued as such until he married Rosario Fresquez of Penasco.

After he was married he practiced carpentry, making coffins for the dead, during the great smallpox plague of the year 1875. There were days in which four or five deaths occurred and Don Manuel could not make coffins enough to supply the demand and there was no other carpenter in Penasco. Some of the dead were placed on poles and dragged to the cemetery by burros.

While the epidemic raged Don Manuel continued making coffins and when it had subsided in Penasco, Don Juan Policarpio sent him to Ocate, Chacon and Santa Clara, now known as Wagon Mound, to make coffins at those places.

In the year 1877 Don Policarpio sent Don Manuel Jesus Vasques in company with other men to the plains on a buffalo hunt. He left Penasco with a Navajo Indian called Juan Jesus Romero, whom Don Policarpio Romero had raised. Alvino Ortega and Jesus Maria Ortega of the settlement of El Llano de San Juan (Plains of Saint John) as well as some thirty other men went with them on the buffalo hunt. They took with them fifteen ox-drawn carts; the oxen's horns were tied securely to the yokes with straps of ox-hide. This group of men met in Penasco on the 15th of November, 1877, before setting out on the hunt.

They set the same day for Mora, there they were joined by more men and more carts, from there they went to Ocate and there also, they were joined by more men and more carts. From this place they traveled as far as the Colorado river which they crossed below what is now the town of Springer in Colfax County. At that time there was not a single house there, or at least they saw none, nor did they see any footprints and there was no trail of any kind.

They were traveling towards the state of Oklahoma and reached Chico, also in Colfax County, New Mexico. At this place they camped for a few days in order to rest their oxen. A meeting was called with the object of placing some one of them at the head of the expedition; votes were cast and Don Alvino Ortega of the Llano de San Juan received a majority of votes and was given the title of "Comandante," Commander.

From this time on nothing was done except at the express command of Don Alvino Ortega; he ordered the oxen to be yoked, he gave the order to make camp, to water the animals, he also ordered mounted men to ride ahead to scout for signs of Indians who might cause them trouble, and to reconnoiter ahead for water for since there was no road over the prairies it was quite possible and dangerous that at any moment they might suddenly come upon a deep canyon or swollen stream which they would not be able to cross. These scouts would ride ahead of the caravan, returning to the camp each night.

They passed close to the site of the city of Clayton by way of a spring called *El Ojo del Cibolo* (Buffalo Spring) and continued across Texas to enter Oklahoma at a point called *Punta de Agua* (Waterhole). It took them a month to reach buffalo country. At a point called Pilares a buffalo bull was killed which furnished them meat for a few days.

From Pilares the expedition traveled for three or four days more until it reached a river called *Rio de las Nutrias* (Beaver River). They camped a short ways down the stream and began hunting buffaloes.

The hunt continued until they had killed enough buffaloes to fill 50 carts with the meat. Only the meat which could be cut into large strips was used, that is, the hind quarters, the hump. The buffalo fat was saved also.

The hunt was conducted on horseback and lances were the weapons used. The commander would order the men to form a line placing the hunters mounted on the swifter horses at each end so that when they advanced on a herd of buffalo the ends of the line would lead the rest in an encircling movement of the beasts.

When the men were formed in line and before they launched themselves on the buffalo the Commander would ask that they all pray together and ask the Almighty God for strength in the impending hunt. When the

Commander was heard to say, "Ave Maria Purissima" (Hail Holy Mary), the line would move forward as one man the end men on their swifter horses outdistancing the rest so as to encircle the herd which was to be attacked.

Some of the men designated as skinners followed the hunt driving burros before them. These men skinned the fat cows only for the dead animals were so plentiful that they would ignore the bulls and lean cows.

They would pack the buffalo meat into camp where they would cut it into convenient sized strips after which they would slice it very thin and hang it up to dry on poles. The "*cecina*" or jerked meat was prepared in the following manner; long strips were cut from the carcasses, for this, men expert at the job were selected. After the meat had cooled it was spread on hides and tramped on until it was drained of blood and then as we have already stated the cecinas were hung on poles to dry in the sun. After it had dried they would stack it up like cord wood, each pile containing enough meat to load three or four carts.

As soon as the Commander thought that sufficient meat had been prepared to fill all of the ox carts he would give orders to cease killing buffaloes. He then would assign three or four carts to each pile of meat and he himself would divide the meat according to the different kinds, larger pieces, meat from the hump and the tallow; the smaller pieces were anybody's property in any quantity desired.

In loading the meat the same method was used as in loading fodder, some would load the meat on the cart while the owner of the cart would trample it down so as to get as much of a load on the cart as he possibly could and all that the oxen would be able to haul home.

After the carts were loaded a party of ten Plains Indians of the Kiowa tribe suddenly rode into camp. The Indians asked for something to eat and their request was complied with, after they had eaten some of the party thought it would be a good idea to kill the Indians arguing that they were only ten in number and could be safely dispatched whereas if they were allowed to leave they might apprise others of their tribe and return in larger numbers to kill the members of the hunting party and steal the meat. Don Manuel Jesus Vasques opposed this plan. The Indians were ordered out of camp. They retired a short distance but followed the homeward bound caravan for a long distance. The following morning on orders of the Commander the long trek home was begun in earnest.

At the crossing of the Nutrias river the ox cart belonging to the only American in the party, became stuck in midstream. This American lived in Ocate. After all the rest of the ox carts had safely crossed the river, all of the party helped in extricating the American's cart from the river and onto dry land. The actual hunting of the buffaloes lasted one month, the trip to and from the hunting grounds required a month's travel each so that the whole trip lasted three months. It took three months of that winter for the entire trip.

This expedition was free of any dispute or fight of any kind, whatever Don Manuel ordered was executed and the whole expedition got along very agreeably.

When Don Manual Jesus Vasquez returned to Penasco preparations were being made for another expedition to the country of the Comanches and Cayguas (Kiowas) towards Kansas. Don Manual Jesus Vasques went on this trip also. The object of this trip was the buying of horses from the Apaches and Kiowas.

On this trip burros loaded with bread were taken along. The bread was a certain kind of bread called Comanche bread. This bread was made of wheat flour but without yeast so that the bread was as hard or harder than a rock; and was traded to the Indians for horses. The Indians were Kiowas and Comanches. A "trinca" of bread was given for each horse. A "trinca" was half a sack of bread or in other words a sack of bread for a pair of horses. At this time the Indians already were receiving some aid from the government and they would feed those who went to trade with them, they had plenty of coffee and sugar. Twenty men went on this trading expedition and they brought fifteen horses back to Penasco with them.

The most of the men who went on this expedition worked for wages, small wages however, no one of them ever made more than 50¢ a day. Yet Don Juan Policarpio Romero never paid Don Manuel Jesus Vasques a single cent for his labors, as shepherd for his flock of goats nor for the making of coffins, nor for his services as a buffalo hunter or horse trader with the Indians, but he did keep Don Manuel and his family. While his patron lived Don Manuel never held one single penny in his hand.

Don Manuel Jesus Vasques who is alive today at the age of 83 says that he never recollects having seen the inside of a school house, but that his patron taught him how to sign his name. Don Juan Policarpio left or designated Don Manuel as one of his heirs and the sons of Don Juan Policarpio Romero gave him four goats and asked him to sign a paper which attested that he had received his share of the inheritance,—and he not knowing how to read signed. The Probate Judge at Taos called him before him and asked Don Manuel if he was content and satisfied and upon his answering that he was, he signed the paper or document.

Source: Interview of Manuel Jesus Vasques. Simeon Tejada, American Life Histories: Manuscripts from the Federal Writers' Project, 1936–1940. Ms. Div., Lib. of Congress. *American Memory.* Lib. of Congress, Washington. August 7, 2008. http://memory.loc.gov/ammem/wpaintro/wpahome.html.

Francisco Trujillo and Billy the Kid

The following is a detailed oral history of William Henry McCarty (1859–1881), alias Wlliam H. Bonney alias Billy the Kid and his involvement in the Lincoln County, New Mexico, War told by Francisco Trujillo, an American of Mexican descent. Trujillo's account places him in close quarters with "the Kid" and provides details of the tensions and alliances among Mexican Americans, Anglo Americans, and Mexican citizens in the Southwest of the late nineteenth century.

I arrived at San Patricio in the year 1877. During the first days of October Sheriff Brady appointed a committee to pursue some bandits whom we found at Harry Baker's ranch at Siete Rios. There we arrested them and brought them to the jail at Lincoln.

In November the people of Penasco, New Mexico went to take the bandits out from jail. Among the people coming from Penasco was Billy the Kid.

At about the same time, my brother, Juan Trujillo, and I went to Pajarito to hunt deer. We were at the mouth of the Pajarito Canyon skinning a deer, when we saw two persons passing. One was Frank Baker, the other was Billy Mote. One was a bandit and the other a body guard whom [the ranch owner] Marfe kept at the ranch. The last one was a thief, also. When they passed my brother said, "Let us get away quickly; these are bad people." So, we got our horses, saddled them and left in the direction of San Patricio. On the way, we met the bandits and the people who were coming from the jail at Lincoln.

The bandits surrounded Juan, my brother. I started to get away, but Billy the Kid followed me telling me to stop. I then turned around and saw that he was pointing a rifle at me so I jumped from my horse and aimed my gun at him. He then went back to where the people were and aimed his gun at Juan saying, "If Francisco does not surrender I am going to kill you." Lucas Gallegos then shouted "Surrender, friend, otherwise they will kill my *compadre* Juan." Billy then took my gun from where I had laid it, and we returned to the place where the people were.

Billy then said to me, "We have exchanged guns now let us exchange saddles." I said that suited me, picking up the gun when another Texan said, "Hand it over you don't need it."

At this point Lucas Gallegos interposed saying to my brother "Let me have the pistol, *compadre*." Then my brother gave Lucas the pistol in its holster. Then and there we parted and left for San Patricio to recount our experiences.

In December, Macky Swin and Marfe went to court about a guardianship and a decision was rendered in favor of Macky Swin. When Marfe saw that he had lost out, he ordered his men to kill Macky Swin or some of his companions. Macky Swin hearing of the order that Marfe had given gathered his people in order to protect himself. Among those he rounded up was Billy the Kid, Charley Barber and Macky Nane. In addition to these three men, six more got together and Macky Swin made them the same promise, to the effect that a prize of $500 was to be awarded to each person who killed one of the Marfes. It was then and there that Billy the Kid organized his people and went out in search of Frank Baker and Billy Mote whom he apprehended on the other side of the Pecos river and brought to Lincoln where it was planned to execute them. Later, when they talked it over further with the rest, it was again decided to kill them, but not to bring them to Lincoln. One of the gang named McLoska said that he preferred to be shot himself rather than to have one of those men killed. No sooner had he said this, when he found himself shot behind the ear. After they killed McLoska, Frank Baker and Billy Mote were promptly executed.

From there Billy's gang left for San Patricio where Billy asked for Francisco Trujillo in order to deliver his gun back to him. It was here that they hired a Mexican boy to go to Lincoln for provisions and to collect the reward that Macky Swin had promised for the Marfes whom they had just killed.

A few days later Macky Nane, Frank Coe and Alex Coe were on their way to Picacho from Lincoln. When they reached the Ojo Ranch they were confronted by the Marfes. They made Frank Coe prisoner and shot Alex Coe in the leg, while the Indian, Juan Armijo, ran after Macky Nane and killed him. By order of Robert Baker, Macky Nane had been the leader whom Macky Swim had had for a guard. Within a few days a complaint was sworn against the Indian, Juan Armijo, and Sheriff Brady deputized Jose Chaves to arrest him. Chaves then named seven men beside himself in order that they should go with him to look for Armijo and he in turn deputized eight Americans and eight Mexicans and altogether they left for Siete Rios where they found Juan across the Pecos river, as well as two other Texans. When Atanasio Martinez, John Scroggin, Billy the Kid and I arrived at the door of the hut, Juan Armijo spoke up and said "How are you Kiko?"

"Come on out" I said to Juan. "You have killed Macky Nane" to which he nodded in assent but adding that it was by order of Robert Baker under threat of being prosecuted himself, should he fail to carry out instructions. I then made my way to Macky Nane who had been hiding behind some tree trunks in an effort to defend himself against those who were shooting at the house, and killed him.

When we left the hut, accompanied by Juan, he said to me "Don't let them kill me Kiko!" Seeing a string of people coming from Siete Rios we ran to a nearby hill and from there towards the plains and then headed for Roswell, on the other side of the Pecos river, and came out two miles below at Gurban. It was here that Billy the Kid, Jose Chaves and Stock proposed to kill the Indian, Armijo.

I said to Chaves, "Is it not better to take him in and let the law have its course?"

Charley Bargar then came up to me and said, "Come on Francisco, let us be running along."

As I came up to Charley, I turned and saw the Indian Armijo riding between them very slowly. When Charley, and after I had gone about 50 yards we noticed that the Indian had gotten away from his captors and was riding away as fast as he could. Billy the Kid and Jose Chaves took out after him and began to shoot at him until they got him. Several of us congregated at the place where he fell.

Billy the Kid then said to me "Francisco, here are the saddle and trappings that I owe you." I then asked them do me the favor of bringing me the horse the Indian Armijo had been riding, in order that I might remove the saddle which was covered with blood. Noting my disgust Doke said that he would take it and clean it and let me have his in the meantime. And so, we exchanged.

Our business finished we turned homeward and crossed the river at a point called "Vado de los Indios." At the New Mexico side of the Pecos river, we slept. In the morning we arose and went to Chisum's to have breakfast. There we found Macky Swin at John Chisum's ranch. Breakfast being over, Macky Swin told us to go into the store and take anything that we wished.

At this point it was decided to leave Captain Stock to guard over Macky Swin. Of the original eight Mexicans in the party, four were left to join the Americans, not having admitted the other four to do so. Macky Swin then asked us to meet him the following Monday at Lincoln because said he, "As soon as I arrive, Brady is going to try and arrest me , and you should not let him get away with it. If I am arrested I shall surely be hung, and I don't want to die, while if you kill Brady you shall earn a reward."

From we left for Berendo where found a *fandango* [dance] in progress. We were enjoying ourselves very thoroughly when don Miguel came up to us and said "Better be on your way boys because presently there will arrive about 50 Marfes who are probably coming here to get you."

Esteco, our leader, agreeing with don Miguel, commanded us to saddle our horses. We had not been gone half a mile when we heard shouts and gun shots so we decided to wait for the gang and have it out. Our efforts were of no avail, however, as the gang failed to show up. We then pursued our course toward the Capitan Mountains and arrived at Agua Negra at day break and there we had our lunch. At this point the party broke up, the Anglos going to Lincoln, the Mexicans to San Patricio whence they arrived on Sunday afternoon.

Billy the Kid then said to Jose Chaves, "Let us draw to see who has to wait for Macky Swin tomorrow at Lincoln. The lots fell to Charley Barber, John Milton and Jim French White, whereupon the leader decided that all nine Anglos should go. Bill thought that it was best for none of the Mexican boys to go and when Chaves protested saying that the Anglos were no braver than he, Bill explained that Brady was married to a Mexican and that it was a matter of policy, all Mexicans being sentimental about their own. Chaves being appeased urged the rest to go on promising to render assistance should a call come for help. A Texan name Doke said that since his family was Mexican too, he would remain with the others. Stock then gave orders to proceed. The horses were saddled and they left for Lincoln. Doke, Fernando Herrera, Jesus Sais and Candelario Hidalgo left for Ruidoso. The next morning dom Pancho Sanches left for Lincoln to make some purchases at the store.

Being in the store about eleven, the mail arrived and with it Macky Swin. There also arrived Brady and a Texan name George Hamilton. At this juncture Brady also arrived where he found Billy the Kid, Jim French, Charley Barber and John Melton. They were in the corral from whence two of the gang shot at one, and two others at the other, where they fell.

Billy the Kid then jumped to snatch Brady's rifle and as he was leaning over someone shot at him from a house they used to call "El Chorro."

Macky Swin then reached the house where the nine of Macky Swin's people were congregated—the four who were in the corral and five who had been at the river. There they remained all day until nightfall and then proceeded to San Patricio.

The next morning they proposed going to the hills should there be a war and so that it could be waged at the edge of town in order not to endanger the lives of the families living there. The same day, toward evening, six Mexicans came to arrest Macky Swin. They did not arrive at the Plaza but camped a little further down between the acequia and the river at a place where there were thick brambles. Shortly after the Mexicans arrived, Macky Swin came with his people to eat supper at the house of Juan Trujillo—that being their headquarters, that also being their mess hall, having hired a man to prepare the meals. After supper they scattered among the different houses, two or three in each house.

In one of these at the edge of town Macky Swin and an American boy whose name was Tome locked themselves in. Next day early in the morning the six Mexicans who had been looking for Macky Swin showed up. When they arrived at the house where Macky Swin was, Tome came out and shot at the bunch of Mexicans and hit Julian, about forty Marfes came down to San Patricio killing horses and chickens. At this point there arrived two

Marfes, an American and a Mexican. The American's name was Ale Cu, and the Mexican's Lucio Montoya. When the Macky Swins became aware of them, they began to fire and killed all the horses. The two Marfes ran away to San Patricio where the rest of the Marfes were tearing down a house and taking out of the store everything that they could get hold of. From there all the Marfes went to Lincoln and for about a month nothing of interest occurred.

I do not recall exactly when Macky Swin, who was being hounded down by the Marfes, was killed but I do remember that he gathered together all his friends and went back home to Lincoln accompanied by eight Mexicans and two Americans, also his wife. When the Marfes found out that he was in the house they surrounded him but seeing that they were unable to hurt him they caused to be brought over a company of soldiers and a cannon from the nearby Fort. Notwithstanding this Macky Swin instructed his people not to fire. For this reason the soldiers had to sit until it was dark. The Marfes then set fire to the house, and the soldiers returned to the fort. When the first room burned down, Ginio Salazar and Ignacio Gonzales came out to the door but the Marfes knocked them down and left them there, dazed. When the flames reached the middle room, an American proposed to go out through the doors of the kitchen on the north side. No sooner did he jump than the Marfes knocked him down. Francisco Samora jumped also and he too was shot. Vincente Romero was next and there the three remained in a heap. It was then proposed by Billy the Kid and Jose Chaves to take aim at the same time and shoot, first to one side then to the other. Chaves took Mack Swin by the arm and told him to go out to which Mack Swin answered by taking a chair and placing it in the corner stating that he would die right there. Billy and Jose Chaves then jumped to the middle door, one on one side, and the other on the other.

Then Robert Bakers and a Texan jumped and said "Here is Macky Swin." Drawing out his revolver he shot him three times in the breast.

When the last shot was fired Billy the Kid said, "Here is Robert," and thrust a revolver in his mouth while Jose Chaves shot at the Texan and hit him in the eye. Billy and Chaves then went along the river headed for San Patricio where they both remained for some time.

In October the Governor accompanied by seven soldiers and other persons came to San Patricio camping. Having heard about the exploits of Billy, the Governor expressed a desire to meet him and sent a messenger to fetch him. The interview was in the nature of a heart-to-heart talk wherein the Governor advised Billy to give up his perilous career. At this point occurred the General Election and George Kimbrall was elected sheriff of the county.

Obeying the Governor's orders he called out the militia having commissioned Sr. Patron as Captain and Billy the Kid as First Lieutenant. During that year—that of '79—things were comparatively quiet and Billy led a very uneventful life.

About the last part of October of the same year, the Governor issued an order that the militia should make an effort to round up all bandits in Chaves county, a task which the militia was not able to accomplish, hence it disbanded. Billy the Kid received an honorable discharge and would probably have gone straight from then on had it not been that at this juncture the District Court met and the Marfes swore a complaint against him and ordered Sheriff Kimbrall to arrest him. Billy stubbornly refused to accompany the sheriff and threatened to take away his life rather than to be apprehended.

Again nothing was heard for a time and then Pat Garrett offered to bring in the desperado for a reward. The Governor having been made aware of the situation himself offered a reward of $500. Immediately Pat Garrett accompanied by four other men got ready to go after Billy and found him and three other boys, whom they surrounded. One morning, during the siege, one of Billy's companions went out to fetch a pail of water whereupon Pat Garrett shot at him, as well as the others, hitting him in the neck and thereby causing him to drop the pail and to run into the house. With a piece of cloth, Billy was able to dress the wound of the injured man and at least stop the hemorrhage. He then advised the wounded man to go out and to pretend to give himself up, hiding his firearm but using it at the first opportune moment to kill Pat. Charley did as we was told but when he went to take aim, dropped dead.

Bill and the other three companions were kept prisoners for three days but finally hunger and thirst drove them out and caused them to venture forth and to give themselves up. Billy was arrested there being no warrant for the others. Then followed the trial which resulted in a sentence to hang within thirty days. News of the execution having spread about people began to come in for miles around to be present on the fatal day but Billy was not to afford them much pleasure having escaped three days before the hanging.

A deputy and jailer had been commissioned to stand guard over him. On the day of the escape at noon the jailer told the deputy to go and eat his dinner and that he would then go himself and fetch the prisoner's. It was while the jailer and Billy remained alone that the prisoner stepped to the window to fetch a paper. He had somehow gotten rid of his handcuffs and only his shackles remained. With the paper in his hand he approached the officer and before the latter knew what his charge was up to, yanked his revolver away from him and the next instant he was dead. Billy lost no time in removing his keeper's cartridge belt as well as a rifle and a "44 W.C.F." (0.44–0.40 Winchester Center-fire, probably a rifle using this caliber shell rifle) which were in the room.

When the deputy heard the shots he thought that the jailer must have shot Billy who was trying to escape and ran from the hotel to the jail on the steps of which he met Billy who said "hello" as he brushed past him, firing at him as he dashed by. Billy's next move was to rush to the hotel and to have Ben Eale remove his shackles. He also provided for him a horse and saddled it for Billy upon the promise that he was to leave it at San Patricio. True to his word Billy secured another horse at San Patricio from his friend Juan Trujillo promising in turn to return the same as soon as he could locate his own.

Billy now left San Patricio and headed for John Chisum's cattle ranch. Among the cowboys there was a friend of Billy Mote who had sworn to kill the Kid whenever he found him in order to avenge his friend. But Billy did not give him time to carry out his plan killing him on the spot.

From there Billy left for Berendo where he remained a few days. Here he found his own horse and immediately sent back Juan Trujillo's. From Berendo Billy left for Puerto de Luna where he visited Juan Patron, his former capitan. Patron did everything to make his and his companion's stay there a pleasant as possible. On the third evening of their stay there was to have been a dance and Billy sent his companion to make a report of what he saw and heard.

While on his way there, and while he was passing in front of some abandoned shacks, Tome was fired upon by one of Pat Garrett's men and killed. No sooner had Billy heard the distressing news than he set out for the house of his friend Pedro Macky at Bosque Grande where he remained in hiding until a Texan named Charley Wilson, and who was supposed to be after Billy, arrived.

The two exchanged greetings in a friendly fashion and then the stranger asked Billy to accompany him to the saloon, which invitation Billy accepted. There were six or seven persons in the saloon when the two entered. Drinks were imbibed in a general spirit of conviviality prevailed when someone suggested that the first one to commit a murder that day was to set the others up. "In that case the drinks are on me," said Charley who commanded all to drink to their heart's content.

Billy then ordered another round of drinks and by this time Charley who was feeling quite reckless began to shoot at the glasses not missing a single one until he came to Billy's. This he pretended to miss, aiming his shot at Bill instead. This gave Billy time to draw out his own revolver and before Charley could take aim again, Billy had shot the other in the breast twice. When he was breathing his last Billy said, "Do not whisper; you were too eager to buy those drinks." It was Billy's turn now to treat the company.

Quiet again reigned for a few days. In the meantime Pat Garrett was negotiating with Pedro Macky for the deliverance of Billy. When all details were arranged for, Pat left for Bosque Grande secretly. At the ranch house, Pedro hid Pat in a room close beside the one Billy was occupying.

Becoming hungry during the night Billy got up and started to prepare a lunch. First he built a fire, then he took his hunting knife and was starting to cut off a hunk of meat from a large piece that hung from one of the rafters

when he heard voices in the adjoining room. Stepping to the door he parti-
ally opened it and thrusting his head in asked Pedro who was with him.

Pedro replied that it was only his wife and asked him to come in. Seeing
no harm in this Billy decided to accept the invitation only to be shot in the
pit of the stomach as he stood in the door. Staggering back to his own room
it was not definitely known that the shot had been fatal until a cleaning
woman stumbled over the dead body upon entering the room, the following
morning.

Source: Interview of "Francisco Trujillo," by Edith Crawford. American Life Histories: Manuscripts from the Federal Writers' Project, 1936–1940. Ms. Div., Lib. of
Congress. *American Memory.* Lib. of Congress, Washington. August 6, 2008. http://
memory.loc.gov/ammem/wpaintro/wpahome.html.

Elfego Baca

Elfego Baca (1865–1945) was a lawman, gunfighter, lawyer, and politician at various points in his life. The Frisco Affair that is mentioned in this reminiscence refers to an incident that took place in Frisco, New Mexico, when Baca was 19. Baca was deputized by the local deputy sheriff to arrest a gang of cowboys who had turned murderous. The ensuing events included a gunfight, an arrest, and the death of one of the men whose horse fell on top of him during the excitement. The arrested cowboy was fined for disorderly conduct, and later Baca was compelled to hold off a reputed eighty cowboys from a refuge in a shack for 36 hours. He survived by lying flat on the dirt floor that had been dug to below ground level. From this legendary event his reputation grew for the next 60 years. In 1958, Disney Studios made a film of his life.

"I never wanted to kill anybody," Elfego Baca told me, "but if a man had it in his mind to kill me, I made it my business to get him first."

Elfego Baca belongs to the six-shooter epoch of American history. Those were the days when hard-shooting Texas cowboys invaded the territory of New Mexico, driving their herds of longhorns over the sheep ranges of the New Mexicans, for whom they had little liking or respect. Differences were settled quickly, with few words and a gun. Those were the days of Billy the Kid, with whom Elfego, at the age of seventeen, made a tour of the gambling joints in Old Albuquerque. In the words of Kyle Crichton, who wrote Elfego Baca's biography, "the life of Elfego Baca makes Billy the Kid look like a piker." Harvey Ferguson calls him "a knight-errant from the romantic point of view if ever the six-shooter West produced one.

And yet Mr. Baca is not a man who lives in his past. "I wonder what I can tell you," he said when I asked him for pioneer stories. "I don't remember so much about those things now. Why don't you read the book Mr. Crichton wrote about me?"

He searched about his desk and brought out two newspaper clippings of letters he had written recently to the *Albuquerque Journal* on local politics. The newspaper had deleted two of the more outspoken paragraphs. Mr. Baca was annoyed.

I tried to draw Mr. Baca away from present day polities to stories of his unusual past, but he does not talk readily about himself, although he seemed anxious to help me. Elfego Baca is a kindly courteous gentleman who is concerned to see that his visitor has the coolest spot in the room.

He brought out books and articles that had been written about him, but he did not seem inclined to reminiscing and answered my questions briefly. "Crichton tells about that in his book" or "Yes, I knew Billy the Kid."

Finally I asked him at random if he knew anything about the famous old Manzano Gang which I had frequently seen mentioned in connection with Torrance County. He replied that he broke up that gang when he was Sheriff of Socorro County.

"There were ten of them," he said, "and I got nine. The only reason I didn't get the other one was that he got over the border and was shot before I got to him. They used to go to a place near Belen and empty the freight cars of grain and one thing and another. Finally they killed a man at La Jolla. Contreros was his name. A very rich man with lots of money in his house, all gold. I got them for that. They were all convicted and sent to the Pen."

Mr. Baca settled back in his chair and made some remark about the late Senator Cutting whose photograph stood on his desk.

I persisted about the Manzano Gang. "I wish you'd tell me more about that gang. How you got them, and the whole story."

"Well," he said, "after that man Contreros was shot, they called me up at my office in Socorro and told me that he was dying. I promised to get the murderers in 48 hours. That was my rule. Never any longer than 48 hours."

Mr. Baca suspected certain men, but when a telephone call to Albuquerque established the fact that they had been in that city at the time of the killing, his next thought was of the Manzano Gang.

Accompanied by two men, he started out on horseback in the direction of La Jolla. Just as the sun was rising; they came to the ranch of Lazaro Cordova. They rode into the stable and found Cordova's son-in-law, Prancasio Saiz, already busy with his horse.

"Good morning," said Elfego, "what are you doing with your horse so early in the morning?"

Saiz replied that he was merely brushing him down a little. Mr. Baca walked over and placed his hand on the saddle. It was wet inside. The saddle blanket was steaming. He looked more closely at the horse. At first sight it had appeared to be a pinto, white with brown spots. Mr. Baca thought he remembered that Saiz rode a white horse.

"What happened to that horse?" he asked.

The man replied that the boys had had the horse out the day before and had painted the spots on him with a kind of berry that makes reddish-brown spots. "Just for a joke," he added.

"Where's your father-in-law?" asked Mr. Baca.

Saiz said that his father-in-law had gone the day before to a fiesta at
La Jolla and had not returned.

"I understand you're a pretty good shot," said Sheriff Baca. "You'd better
come along, and help me round up some men I'm after for the killing of
Contreros in La Jolla."

Saiz said that he had work to do on the ranch, but at the insistence of
Mr. Baca, he saddled his horse and rode out with the three men.

"About as far as from here to the station," went on Mr. Baca, "was a
graveyard where the gang was supposed to camp out. I rode over to it and
found where they had lunched the day before. There were sardine cans and
cracker boxes and one thing and another. Then I found where one of them
had had a call to nature. I told one of my men to put it in a can. Saiz did
not know about this, and in a little while he went over behind some
mesquite bushes and had a call to nature. After he came back I sent my
man over, and by God it was the same stuff—the same beans and red chili
seeds! So I put Saiz under arrest and sent him back to the jail at Socorro with
one of my deputies, although he kept saying he couldn't see what I was
arresting him for."

Mr. Baca and his other deputy proceeded in the direction of La Jolla.
Before long they saw a man on horseback coming toward them.

"He was running that horse like everything. When we met I saw that he
was a Texan. Doc Something or other was his name. I can't remember
now. But he was a pretty tough man."

"You a Sheriff?" he said to Mr. Baca.

"No," replied Mr. Baca, "no, I'm not a Sheriff. Don't have nothing to do
with the law, in fact."

"You're pretty heavily armed," remarked the man suspiciously.

"I generally arm myself this way when I go for a trip in the country,"
answered Baca, displaying his field glasses. "I think it's safer."

"Well, if you want fresh horses, you can get them at my ranch, a piece
down the road," said the Texan.

Mr. Baca figured that this was an attempt to throw him off the trail, so as
soon as the Texan was out of sight, he struck out east over the mountains for
Manzano. Just as he was entering the village he saw two of the gang coming
down the hill afoot leading their horses. He placed them under arrest and
sent them back to Socorro with his other deputy.

It was about two o'clock in the morning when Mr. Baca passed the
Cordova ranch again on his way back. He roused Lazaro Cordova, who
had returned from La Jolla by that time, and told him to dress and come
with him to Socorro.

"The old man didn't want to come," said Mr. Baca, "and kept asking
'what you want with me anyhow?' I told him that he was under arrest,
and on the way to Socorro I told him that unless he and his son-in-law came
across with a complete statement about the whole gang, I would hang both

of them, for I had the goods on them and knew all right that they were both in on the killing of Contreros. I put him in the same cell with his son-in-law, and told him it was up to him to bring Saiz around. They came through with the statement. I kept on catching the rest of the gang, until I had them all. All but the one who got himself shot before I caught up with him."

"If you ever go to Socorro you ask Billy Newcomb, the Sheriff down there now to show you the records. You might see the place on the way down where they buried a cowboy I shot. It's a little way off the main road though.

"That was a long time before I was a real Sheriff. In those days I was a self-made deputy. I had a badge I made for myself, and if they didn't believe I was a deputy, they'd better believe it, because I made 'em believe it.

"I had gone to Escondida a little way from Socorro to visit my uncle. A couple of Texas cowboys had been shooting up the town of Socorro. They hadn't hurt anybody that time. Only frightened some girls. That's the way they did in those days—ride through a town shooting at dogs and cats and if somebody happened to get in the way—powie!—too bad for him. The Sheriff came to Escondida after them. By that time they were making a couple of Mexicans dance, shooting up the ground around their feet. The Sheriff said to me 'Baca, if you want to help, come along, but there's going to be shooting.'

"We rode after them and I shot one of them about three hundred yards away. The other got away—too many cottonwood trees in the way.

"Somebody asked me what that cowboy's name was. I said I didn't know. He wasn't able to tell me by the time I caught up with him."

I asked what the Sheriff's name was, and when Mr. Baca said it was Pete Simpson, I said, "The one you were electioneering for the time of the Frisco affair when you held off about 80 cowboys for over 36 hours." This is the one of Mr. Baca's exploits that has been most frequently written about.

"Hell, I wasn't electioneering for him," he said. "I don't know where they got that idea. I couldn't have made a speech to save my life. And I didn't wear a Prince Albert coat either. They didn't have such things in this country in those days."

"Is it true that you ate dinner afterward with French and some other men who had been shooting at you, and talked the affair over," I asked.

"I ate dinner with some men afterward but I don't remember who they were now. I don't think that man French was there at all, although he must have been in the neighborhood, as he seemed to know all about it. But I don't remember him. Jim Cook was one that was shooting at me though. He was a pretty tough man, but he came near getting it."

He showed me a photograph which Jim Cook had sent him recently. The picture showed an old man who still looks as though he could not be easily trifled with. It was inscribed, "To Elfego Baca in memory of that day at Frisco."

"Did you see the letter that Englishman wrote to Crichton? He wanted to hang me. 'Why don't you hang that little Mexican so-and-so?' he asked.

I said, 'Why don't you be the one to do it?' and pulled my guns, and wooo, he wasn't so eager. You know I surrendered only on condition that I keep my guns. They placed six guards over me, but they rode 25 steps ahead of me all the way to Socorro.

"Those were great old days. Everything is very quiet now, isn't it?" said Mr. Baca looking up. "I think I'll run for something this fall, but I don't know what yet."

Source: "Interview of Elfego Baca," Janet Smith. American Life Histories: Manuscripts from the Federal Writers' Project, 1936–1940. Ms. Div., Lib. of Congress. *American Memory*. Lib. of Congress, Washington. August 6, 2008. http:// memory.loc.gov/ammem/wpaintro/wpahome.html.

Sunday Seven

The following tale of the punishment meted out for greed and deceit is popular not only in the Hispanic Southwest. Variations of the plot are found in the European forms from which this narrative is derived, in the Middle East, and in Japan where the troublesome affliction is a facial cyst rather than a hump on the back.

Long ago there were two hunchbacks. One was kind but the other was mean and spiteful. The two hunchbacks could not work in the village because everybody made fun of them; therefore, they went into the hills to cut wood. That is, the kind one cut all the wood since the mean and spiteful one was very lazy and was always telling his companion, "Ay, how sick I am today! It is better if you go and cut the wood this week." His partner, being kindhearted, would go into the mountains and do all the work week after week.

One day, when the mean one had stayed at home as usual, the good woodcutter worked very hard and was very tired. Since his house was far away, he decided to camp near a small spring. About midnight, the woodcutter heard someone singing. At first he thought that somebody had camped nearby but when he had listened to what was being sung, he realized that the voices he heard were not human.

Very cautiously he arose and silently walked to the place where the singing came from. Imagine his surprise when he saw a group of fairies singing and dancing around a blazing fire.

Monday and Tuesday and Wednesday three,
Monday and Tuesday and Wednesday three.

That was all the fairies sang, they repeated the same line over and over again. It seemed that it was the only song they knew. The woodcutter then decided that he would talk to them. Naturally, as soon as he heard them singing again, he went near the fire and the fairies saw him at once.

"What do you want, oh mortal?" asked the fairies. "Why do you come to bother us?"

"Because I can help you. Listen to me and you will see that your song will sound better this way." Then he sang:

> *Monday and Tuesday and Wednesday three,*
> *Thursday and Friday and Saturday six.*

Oh! The fairies were filled with joy. They noticed then that the good woodcutter was a hunchback. They told him to kneel down and with a magic wand touched his hump. Immediately it disappeared, leaving him strong and strong.

Suddenly, the earth began to tremble; the rocks began to shake, all with a terrifying sound.

"It is the ogres who come! Quickly!" the fairies told the woodcutter. "Climb that tree; otherwise the ogres will kill you." And the fairies disappeared.

Quick as the wink of an eye, the woodcutter climbed the tree and hid in it foliage. No sooner had the woodcutter settled himself than three ugly and huge ogres sat themselves at the base of the tree and began to chat.

"Well, *amigos,* what evil deeds have you performed during the year?" Thus they asked each other.

"Well," said one of the ogres, "I have blinded the entire village. And so blind are they, that not even the sun can they see."

They all laughed and poked each other in the ribs.

The second ogre then said, "Ha! you think that was work? I have condemned the people of my kingdom to silence. And so dumb are they that even the children are unable to cry."

The ogres laughed louder than before.

"Well, *señores,*" said the third, "I haven't been idle either. I have made my people so deaf that they cannot even hear the cries of the souls in purgatory."

And the ogres laughed more loudly than ever, rolling on the ground with merriment. They were so evil that all human miseries caused them joy. The poor woodcutter, hearing them speak thus, trembled with horror.

"However," said the ogre who had spoken first, "if you have done as I have, then everything proceeds well. Those poor unfortunates whom I have blinded don't know how easily they can be cured. Nevertheless, don't think I am going to cure, much less give them the remedy."

"Good," said the second ogre. "You are going to tell us, no? I also have a remedy to cure the deafness of my people and I am sure that our friend here has also a remedy for the dumbness of his people."

"You are right," answered the third ogre, "I also have a remedy."

"*Señores,*" said the first, "to cure the blindness of my subjects all one has to do is to collect the dew during the first week of April. Then by rubbing a finger dipped in this dew over the eyes of the blind, they will be cured."

"You must guard your secret well; it is very ingenious." exclaimed the second ogre. "But listen to my remedy. As I have told you, I have deafened my subjects. Do you know how they can be cured? It is certainly more difficulty to cure this deafness than the blindness you spoke of. You have heard of the Hill of the Bells; all one has to do is take the person who is afflicted with deafness to this Hill, place him next to the rock, and then strike this rock with a hammer. The sound resulting from the blow will cure the deaf person."

"That is nothing," said the third ogre. "To cure the dumbness of my people, one must go into the fields and pick flowers from the *cenizo* plant, which blooms only after a good rain. These flowers are set to boil, and a tea is made from them. The afflicted is given this tea to drink. Then not only is he cured of dumbness, but of every known ailment."

The ogres were enjoying themselves a great deal, but since dawn was approaching, they agreed to meet again at the same place a year from that date.

As soon as the ogres left, the woodcutter clambered down from the tree saying to himself, "since the fairies have been kind to me, I will repay kindness with kindness. I will go and cure those poor afflicted persons the ogres talked about. However, since it is a long time until April, I will first go and cure the deaf and the dumb."

Walking, walking, the woodcutter finally reached the land of the dumb. The good man picked the *cenizo* flowers, brewed the tea, and gave it to the dumb. Immediately their speech was restored. So grateful were all these people that they loaded the woodcutter's little donkey with bars of gold and silver. From the land of the dumb, the woodcutter traveled to the kingdom of the deaf. He took the deaf to the Hill of the Bells and cured them. *Dios mio!* What joy! These people also gave the woodcutter a donkey loaded with gold and silver bars. Since April was near, the woodcutter traveled to the country of the blind. Camping on a grass-covered prairie, he waited for the first week of April When the proper time arrived, the good woodcutter collected the dew from the grass, entered the village of the blind, and cured all. As a reward, the previously blind loaded their benefactor with still more gold and silver.

At last he returned to his home, where his friend the envious hunchback awaited him. The good woodcutter related his adventures, but the evil one did not care about the gold or the silver. He wanted to rid his back of its hump.

"*Compadre,*" the evil one would ask his good friend, "why don't you tell me where this tree is? The ogres will be there soon; maybe I can also be rich like you. But above all, I hope the fairies will straighten my back."

The kindhearted woodcutter took pity on his friend and agreed to do as he asked. On the morning of the day set for the meeting of the ogres, the good woodcutter took his friend to the tree. The mean hunchback, without even thanking his kind companion, climbed the tree and set himself to await the arrival of the ogres and the fairies.

Before the fairies arrived, the earth and the rocks trembled as in the previous occasion and the ogres met under the tree.

"*Amigos,*" said the largest ogre, "there is a traitor amongst us. Someone has cured the blindness of my subjects. We were the only ones who know what was said here a year ago; it must be one of us."

"It wasn't I," said the second, "because in my kingdom the dumb can now talk."

"And my previously deaf people can now hear," called in anger the third. "A woodcutter came to my kingdom and cured everyone."

"He was the one that cured my subjects!" exclaimed the other two ogres.

The fairies appeared then, singing and dancing. Their fear of the ogres was forgotten.

> *Monday and Tuesday and Wednesday three*
> *Thursday and Friday and Saturday six.*

The hunchback, who had seen the fairies come out, was impatient to add to the song, hoping that his hump would be removed. When the fairies reached the word "six" the hunchback yelled the first thing that came to his mind:

> *"And Sunday seven!"*

For an instant the ogres and the fairies stood as if carved from stone. Recovering their faculties in an instant, the fairies exclaimed, "Our song has been ruined!" Then they disappeared.

The ogres by this time had also looked around. Yelling "There is the traitor!" they reached into the tree and brought down the hunchback.

"And so it was you, insignificant spider, who revealed our secrets! Well, take this!" And the ogres decorated the back of the hunchback with another hump.

Source: "Domingo Siete," Gabriel A. Cordova Jr. "Magic Tales of Mexico," M.A. Thesis. Texas Western College, El Paso, TX, 1951. http://www.genecowan.com/magictales/, retrieved August 6, 2008.

The Bird of the Sweet Song

"The Bird of the Sweet Song" is based on the efforts of a blind man's son to restore his father's sight. Embarking on the first quest, the man's son forfeits the supernatural aid he gains from a dead man's spirit by his own lack of discipline. The man's youngest daughter, true to the general European folktale pattern, eventually succeeds in restoring her father's sight, but at great sacrifice. Unlike most such tales in the Latino tradition, there is no "happily ever after."

Once there was an old man who was blind, and the sorcerers whom he consulted told him that the only thing which would cure his blindness was a certain sweet-voiced bird. So his son started out to find the bird. Soon he came to a rancho, where he found a dead man who had no one to bury him. Feeling reverence for the dead, he sought a man to attend the corpse, and then sent for a priest to bury him. The priest inquired of the messenger whether he came on his own business or for another, remarking that it were better if the other should himself come to present his requests. Nevertheless he went, and the corpse was buried with the proper rites. Then the boy went on his way.

Soon afterwards he met in the road the spirit of the dead man to whom he had given the charity of burial. It had assumed the form of a Fox, who asked him where he was going, and why. He replied that he was going to the country of the Moors to fetch the bird of the sweet song. Then the Fox told him that it was very near, and that he would give him a horse to assist him. The Fox knew whether the horse was given pasture or not. He further advised him that if he should find the Moors with their eyes open, it was a sign that they were sleeping, but that if their eyes were closed, then he should know that they were wide awake. But the Fox warned him that he must not carry away any of the beautiful maidens which he would find in the house of the Moors.

Soon the boy arrived at the castle of the Moors, and entered. There he found the Moors with their eyes open, and by this he knew that they were sleeping. Many birds were there in beautiful cages; but he passed these by, and took a plain, common cage in which was a homely bird, for he knew that this was the bird of the sweet song. Likewise he seized one of the beautiful maidens, contrary to the Fox's orders, mounted a wooden horse which he found there, and flew through the window.

Then the Moors awakened, and pursued them, and soon overtook them. They carried the boy and the maiden back to their castle, and imprisoned them there. Soon the Fox reappeared to him, and said, "You did not do as I instructed you." He then told him that the maiden was in the garden and would speak to no one, and that the bird refused to sing, but that he had gone for some charcoal, and begged permission of the Moors to give her two pieces. Then she at once began to talk, the bird to sing, and the horse to neigh.

Soon afterward the boy again seized the maiden and the bird, mounted the horse, and flew away. Again the Fox reappeared, warning them not to cross the river with the bargemen, for, should they attempt to do so, they would never reach the other shore; but, disregarding the warning, they kept on until they came to the river where they met the bargemen. These said that they did not have room for all to cross at once, but that they would first cross with the maiden, the bird, and the horse, and later return for the boy. The girl, bird, and horse were safely landed on the other shore, and the bargemen then returned for the boy; but when they reached the middle of the river, the boat was upset. Now, it happened that there was a sabino tree in the middle of the river, and the boy held tightly to this.

Then suddenly the Fox appeared on the river bank, and told him to hold tight until he made a rope. So he began to pull the hairs out of his tail, and twisted them to form a rope. When it was long enough, he threw it out to the boy, and told him to tie it about his waist, so that he might pull him ashore. Reaching the shore, the boy went sadly home, leaving the bird of the sweet song, the maiden and the horse, on the other side of the river.

When the blind father heard that his son had lost the bird of the sweet song, he again went to the sorcerers, who told him that the sole remedy now for his blindness was to bathe in the sea every afternoon. The first day that he went there, an ugly Worm appeared, and told him that if he would give him one of his three daughters, he would cure his infirmity.

Returning, he told his daughters of this, and they agreed, that, if the Worm would cure their father, one of them would go with the Worm. So the next afternoon the old man took his eldest daughter; but when she saw the Worm, she was horrified, and said that she would never go with such an ugly creature. The next afternoon when the blind father went to bathe, he took his second daughter; but she likewise refused to go when she saw the ugliness of the Worm. Now, only the youngest remained, but she said that she would gladly do anything if only her father might be cured. So she went with him the next afternoon when he went to bathe. Then the ugly Worm appeared, and asked her if she were willing to go with him. Turning to her father, she asked him to give her his blessing. Then from the sea there came a great wave which carried the maiden and the Worm out to sea with it.

Source: Adapted from "The Bird of the Sweet Song," J. Alden Mason, "Four Mexican-Spanish Fairy-Tales from Azqueltan, Jalisco," *Journal of American Folklore* 25 (1912): 191–198, pp. 195–196.

The Louse Skin Coat

The test of answering an obscure riddle to win the hand of a princess is a common folktale motif. The enigma is generally solved by a humble figure, such as the shepherd in this tale, who happens upon the solution to the riddle by uncovering a hidden bit of information. In this tale, the social difference between the princess and the shepherd is emphasized by the fact that the ingestion of royal blood causes the louse from whom the king's coat is made to grow to fantastic proportions. The overall theme of this short tale focuses on bridging of the gap between commoner and royalty.

Once there was a king who had a daughter. One day when the queen was combing her daughter's hair, the mother found a louse.

"Look, Father," said the princess, "at the louse Mother found in my hair."

"Don't kill it!" exclaimed the king. "Let us put it in a jar. I am curious to find how large a louse can grow when it feeds on royal blood."

The king placed the louse in a jar and every day he would let the louse feed on the royal blood of the princess. He would let the louse suck on the skin of the girl for several hours. The louse grew so large that the king had to place it in a bigger jar. It kept on growing until finally the king placed it in a barrel. The princess kept on feeding it until it became so large that the king placed it in a tun [a large cask commonly used for holding beer or wine]. When the louse could not be kept in the tun, the king killed it. Then he had the louse skin tanned and ordered the royal tailor to make a coat from it.

When the coat was made, the king put it on and asked everybody the same question: "Can you guess the name of the animal from which the skin of my coat was taken?"

Some said it was from a steer, others from a deer, but none could guess rightly.

Finally, the king proclaimed throughout his kingdom that anyone solving the riddle of the coat would be wed to the princess.

From everywhere people came to try to solve the riddle, but none could guess correctly.

One day a *pastor* [shepherd] came with his flock to the city. He was going to market to sell his sheep, but decided that he might do well to go and see the sights. After walking a long while, he arrived at the outskirts of the king's palace. Being tired, the pastor rolled a cigarette and had just leaned against the wall of the king's garden to smoke when he heard voices. It was the king talking to his wife: "I don't think anybody is going to guess that my coat is made from a louse-skin."

As soon as he heard this, the shepherd left, thinking, "Now I will be able to marry the princess."

Next day, the pastor went to the palace and asked for an audience with the king. When he was before the king, the shepherd said, "Señor, I have come to see if I can solve the riddle of your coat."

"Guess," said the king.

"Señor," said the pastor, "the coat is made from a louse-skin."

"You have guessed!" cried the king.

So the king ordered that the marriage of the shepherd and the princess take place without delay.

Source: "The Louse Skin Coat," Gabriel A. Cordova Jr. "Magic Tales of Mexico," M.A. Thesis. Texas Western College, El Paso, TX, 1951. http://www.genecowan.com/magictales/, retrieved August 6, 2008.

THE SUPERNATURAL

Princess Papantzin's Resurrection

Montezuma II, also spelled Moctezuma, ruled the Aztec Empire from 1502 to 1520 at the time of the arrival of Hernan Cortés and his Spanish conquistadores. The resurrection and prophecies of Princess Papantzin was one of the cataclysmic signs alleged to have appeared to herald the conquest of the Aztecs by Spanish forces. In spite of the claims at the beginning of the following narrative, the historical validity of this account may be questionable because of the bias of the non-Aztec chroniclers of the event. The prophecy was included in English author H. Rider Haggard's (1856–1929) novel, Montezuma's Daughter.

One of the weirdest legends in Mexican tradition recounts how Papantzin, the sister of Montezuma II, returned from her tomb to prophesy to her royal brother concerning his doom and the fall of his empire at the hands of the Spaniards. On taking up the reins of government Montezuma had married this lady to one of his most illustrious servants, the governor of Tlatelulco, and after his death it would appear that she continued to exercise his almost vice regal functions and to reside in his palace.

In course of time she died, and her obsequies were attended by the emperor in person, accompanied by the greatest personages of his court and kingdom. The body was interred in a subterranean vault of his own palace, in close proximity to the royal baths, which stood in a sequestered part of the extensive grounds surrounding the royal residence. The entrance to the vault was secured by a stone slab of moderate weight, and when the numerous ceremonies prescribed for the interment of a royal personage had been completed the emperor and his suite retired.

At daylight next morning one of the royal children, a little girl of some six years of age, having gone into the garden to seek her governess, espied the Princess Papan standing near the baths. The princess, who was her aunt, called to her, and requested her to bring her governess to her. The child did as she was bid, but her governess, thinking that imagination had played her a trick, paid little attention to what she said. As the child persisted in her statement, the governess at last followed her into the garden, where she saw Papan sitting on one of the steps of the baths. The sight of the supposed dead princess filled the woman with such terror that she fell down in a swoon.

The child then went to her mother's apartment, and detailed to her what had happened. She at once proceeded to the baths with two of her attendants, and at sight of Papan was also seized with affright. But the princess reassured her, and asked to be allowed to accompany her to her apartments, and that the entire affair should for the present be kept absolutely secret.

Later in the day she sent for Tiçotzicatzin, her majordomo, and requested him to inform the emperor that she desired to speak with him immediately on matters of the greatest importance. The man, terrified, begged to be excused from the mission, and Papan then gave orders that her uncle Nezahualpilli, King of Tezcuco, should be communicated with.

That monarch, on receiving her request that he should come to her, hastened to the palace. The princess begged him to see the emperor without loss of time and to entreat him to come to her at once. Montezuma heard his story with surprise mingled with doubt. Hastening to his sister, he cried as he approached her: "Is it indeed you, my sister, or some evil demon who has taken your likeness?"

"It is I indeed, your Majesty," she replied. Montezuma and the exalted personages who accompanied him then seated themselves, and a hush of expectation fell upon all as they were addressed by the princess in the following words, "Listen attentively to what I am about to relate to you. You have seen me dead, buried, and now behold me alive again. By the authority of our ancestors, my brother, I am returned from the dwellings of the dead to prophesy to you certain things of prime importance.

"At the moment after death I found myself in a spacious valley, which appeared to have neither commencement nor end, and was surrounded by lofty mountains. Near the middle I came upon a road with many branching paths. By the side of the valley there flowed a river of considerable size, the waters of which ran with a loud noise. By the borders of this I saw a young man clothed in a long robe, fastened with a diamond, and shining like the sun, his visage bright as a star. On his forehead was a sign in the figure of a cross. He had wings, the feathers of which gave forth the most wonderful and glowing reflections and colors. His eyes were as emeralds, and his glance was modest. He was fair, of beautiful aspect and imposing presence. He took me by the hand and said: 'Come hither. It is not yet time for you to cross the river. You possess the love of God, which is greater than you know or can comprehend.' He then conducted me through the valley, where I espied many heads and bones of dead men. I then beheld a number of black folk, horned, and with the feet of deer. They were engaged in building a house, which was nearly completed. Turning toward the east for a space, I beheld on the waters of the river a vast number of ships manned by a great host of men dressed differently from ourselves. Their eyes were of a clear grey, their complexions ruddy, they carried banners and ensigns in their hands and wore helmets on their heads. They called themselves 'Sons of the Sun.' The youth who conducted me and caused me to see all these things said that it was not yet the will of the gods that I should cross the river, but that I was to be reserved to behold the future with my own eyes, and to enjoy the benefits of the faith which these strangers brought with them; that the bones I beheld on the plain were those of my countrymen who had died in ignorance of that faith, and had consequently suffered great torments; that the house being built by the black folk was an edifice prepared for those who would fall in battle with the seafaring strangers whom I had seen; and that I was destined to return to my compatriots to tell them of the true faith, and to announce to them what I had seen that they might profit thereby."

Montezuma hearkened to these matters in silence, and felt greatly troubled. He left his sister's presence without a word, and, regaining his own apartments, plunged into melancholy thoughts.

Papantzin's resurrection is one of the best authenticated incidents in Mexican history, and it is a curious fact that on the arrival of the Spanish Conquistadores one of the first persons to embrace Christianity and receive baptism at their hands was the Princess Papan.

Source: Spence, Lewis. *The Myths of Mexico and Peru* (London: G. G. Harrap and Company, 1913), pp. 139–142.

Clemencia and José

According to folklorist Gabriel A. Cordova Jr., this tale, although well known in oral tradition, had not been documented by an academic prior to 1951. Tension is created in the plot between the Catholic piety of Clemencia and the evil of her witch mother (see "Three Live Witches" and "Witch Tales from New Mexico" for additional background on the nature of witches in Latino folklore). The motif of the escape assisted by magical objects is common in the world's cultures. The fact that Clemencia also displays magical powers is worth noting. The concept of positive magic, for example to heal, persists in many segments of traditional Latino culture.

Very long ago there lived a couple who had a daughter named Clemencia.

The mother, who was a witch, did not like Clemencia because she said the girl was a fool who was always going to church.

One day, the crops were more abundant than usual and Clemencia's father was forced to hire a youth named José to help with the harvesting. In a short time, José and Clemencia fell in love and wanted to marry as soon as possible.

When they asked for her parents' approval, the father gave his permission, but the witch denied it.

Nevertheless, Clemencia and José fell more and more in love with each other, thus increasing the anger the witch bore them.

One day when José was in the corral taking care of the mules, the mother decided to kill him, hoping to end the love affair and make Clemencia suffer. The witch went in search of her husband and said to him, "Old man, tell José to go to the pasture and bring back the black mule that is grazing there."

Clemencia, when she heard her mother say this, guessed that the witch was trying to kill her loved one.

"Look, José, shortly my father will come to tell you to bring a black mule from the pasture and put it in the corral. That black mule is my mother. If you ride her, she will buck; and if she unseats you, she will kill you. So listen closely to what I am going to tell you. When you mount the mule and she starts to buck, bend over and bite her right ear. This will render her powerless. Bring the mule and put it in the corral but be careful not to tell anybody anything."

Everything happened exactly as Clemencia had predicted. José rendered the mule powerless and brought her safely to the corral. When it was time for supper, José noticed that the old woman was wearing a bandage on her right ear.

That night Clemencia and José decided to elope. They agreed that at eleven Clemencia would wake José and both would flee.

At eleven Clemencia went to José's bedroom. She shook him awake and said, "Spit on your bed, I have already spat on mine." Then they left.

Soon after, the old witch awoke and began calling Clemencia, but the spittle the daughter had left on her bed answered, "Mother?"

The old woman, hearing Clemencia's voice, went back to sleep. A long time went by and Clemencia's mother woke again. She called Clemencia again but this time there was no answer. The spittle had dried. The angered witch got up and went to Clemencia's bedroom. Not finding the girl there, she ran toward José's bedroom. She did not find him either. Guessing what had happened, the witch waited for daylight, then turned herself into an eagle and flew in search of the youths. After flying a long while, the witch saw them. Clemencia also saw the eagle and knew it was her mother. Clemencia, who had learned a good deal of magic from her mother, dropped a comb on the ground, whereupon in a moment a huge forest sprang up. The eagle could not fly over it so she came down to earth and changed back into the witch. With counter-magic she made the forest disappear. Then she turned into an eagle once more and continued her pursuit of the lovers.

José and Clemencia had gained some ground but soon noticed that the eagle was almost upon them again. The girl then threw down a mirror which became a lake so broad that the eagle could not fly over it.

Seeing the huge size of the lake, the eagle landed, became a witch again, and caused the lake to disappear. Trying her magic again, she turned back into an eagle and flew in pursuit. Again the eagle saw the couple, but Clemencia threw a handful of ashes in the air. The ashes turned into a dense fog which the eagle could not cross. As it was getting dark, the witch could not follow the lovers any more. The witch lost her powers with the setting of the sun. Before flying home, however, the witch cursed the lovers saying, "Bad daughter, remember that your lover will leave you as soon as you arrive at the first village."

Clemencia and José did not pay attention but kept on without stopping to rest. At last they came to a village. As they neared the outskirts of the town, Clemencia sat down to rest because she was very tired and because her shoes were torn from walking so much.

"Wait here for me while I go into the village and buy you a pair of shoes and something to eat," said José.

Clemencia did not want José to leave her, but he insisted so much that she let him go.

It grew dark and José did not return. Another day went by, and he still did not return. Finally, remembering her mother's curse, Clemencia went into the village, crying all the way.

Failing to find her lover, Clemencia had to go to work. One day when she was feeling more sad than usual two doves flew down to her window. It seemed that they were trying to cheer Clemencia as they cooed and cooed.

Clemencia captured the doves and patiently taught them many tricks. Thus several weeks went by, and when the doves had learned their tricks well, Clemencia took them to the city square where they began to perform.

Many people came to see and admire the clever stunts the doves could do. Clemencia meanwhile kept a sharp eye out for José, always trying to locate him in the crowd. Finally, one day she saw José, but he did not recognize her. She then touched the female dove with a wand and the bird began walking in circles around the male, saying all the while: "Currucutucu, currucutucu, do you remember when you used to tell me that you loved me?"

"No!" the male would answer.

"Do you remember," the little dove asked, "that we left my home? Do you remember that you left me by the road?"

"No!" the pigeon would answer.

"Do you remember that you left me by the road, because you went for some shoes that I could wear when we entered the village?"

The pigeon exclaimed, "Yes! I remember now."

At the same time José, who had been watching, said, "I also remember now. You are my Clemencia, my love." And taking Clemencia in his arms, José told her that they would never part. So they were married and lived happily for many, many years.

Source: "Clemencia and José," Gabriel A. Cordova Jr. "Magic Tales of Mexico," M.A. Thesis. Texas Western College, El Paso, TX, 1951http://www.genecowan .com/magictales/, retrieved August 6, 2008.

The Giant's Secret

According to the standard classification system for folktales developed by Antti Aarne and Stith Thompson, the following tale is categorized as "The Ogre's (Devil's) Heart in the Egg." In this classification system, characters may change (for example, a giant is substituted for an ogre), but basic plot elements remain the same. Using this method of comparison, the story of "The Giant's Secret" has been collected throughout Europe. On the other hand, there seem to be no versions native to the Americas. For this reason, the following folktale plot appears to be borrowed from European folklore and adapted, by the inclusion of the coyote as a pivotal character, to the American Southwest.

Long ago there was a king who had a very brave son. One day the son told his father, "Father, I am going to roam the world in search of adventures."

The king did not want to grant his son permission to do so, but the prince insisted so much that the king finally consented.

The prince mounted a beautiful horse and journeyed seeking adventures. After traveling a long, long way, he came to a forest which he had to cross. Penetrating the deep woods, he suddenly heard a hound bay and a lion roar. Then he saw four animals: a lion, a hound, an eagle and an ant, all of them arguing over the carcass of a deer.

Seeing the prince approach, the lion roared, "One moment, *hombre*. As you see, all of us argue because we cannot decide which part of this dead deer belongs to each. If you make a satisfactory division of the carcass amongst us, we will reward you."

The prince agreed and divided the deer into four parts. To the lion he gave the haunches, to the hound the ribs, to the eagle the entrails, and to the ant the head.

The animals agreed to the division as the lion said to the prince, "We promised to reward you and we will keep that promise." Pulling a hair from its mane and giving it to the prince, the lion continued, "Take this hair. Whenever you want to become a lion just say 'God and Lion' and you will be transformed into a lion. To become a man again, all you have to say is 'God and Man.'"

The hound also gave the prince a hair from its body and told him to effect his transformation into a hound, he had only to change the wording of the phrase to "God and Hound," then "God and Man."

The eagle then gave the prince a feather and told him to say, "God and Eagle," in order to become an eagle. The ant also gave the prince one of its antennae, telling the youth to say "God and Ant" to become an ant.

The prince thanked the animals and went on his way, until one day he came to a castle which appeared to be deserted. The prince desired to see the interior of this castle, but it seemed impossible as the place was completely surrounded by a high wall. He then remembered the gifts he had received from the animals in the forest. Pulling out the feather, the prince said, "God and Eagle." He turned into an eagle and flew over the castle. In the highest tower of the castle he saw an open window, to which he flew and stopped on the sill. He looked into a bedroom and there saw a beautiful maiden asleep.

The prince then said, "God and Man," and turning into a man again, entered the bedroom the better to see the sleeping maiden.

The maiden awoke and, seeing the prince bending over her, asked, "Señor, what do you want here? If the giant, owner of this castle, finds you, he will kill you without mercy."

"Señora," answered the prince, "I do not fear the giant, since I seek adventure. As far as I can see, you seem to be a prisoner in this huge castle. If I can be of service, please order me to do what I can."

"True," said the maid, "I am a prisoner of the giant. But it is hopeless to ask for your aid. The giant conquers all who fight against him."

Suddenly a thundering voice was heard echoing through the castle. The maiden exclaimed, "We are lost! The giant will be here any moment and there is no place where you can hide."

"Do not be afraid, señora," and holding the little ant's antenna the prince said the magic words which made him an ant.

At that instant the giant came in saying, "Señora, I am sure that you were talking to someone." The giant searched everywhere but did not see the ant. Satisfied, he left.

The prince then said, "God and Man," and became a man again.

The maiden was so happy she could not even talk, but finally she spoke to the prince.

"Señor, perhaps you can save me. But to do so, you have to slay the giant, and to slay the giant you must first break the egg in which the giant's life is kept. That egg is very well hidden. Nobody has ever been able to find it."

The following day the giant came to the maiden's bedroom and the girl said, "Señor, last night I dreamt that your life was in danger. A man was breaking the egg which hides your secret."

"Do not worry, señora, that egg is very well hidden," he replied.

The giant left, but nevertheless he worried. Perhaps his life was really in danger. Quick as the wink of an eye, the giant became a pigeon which flew out of the window.

The prince, who had been watching the giant all this time, said, "God and Eagle" and began to fly in pursuit of the pigeon.

The pigeon landed at a cave from which it took a little box containing an egg. At this particular moment the eagle arrived. The pigeon, seeing the eagle, changed into a coyote who swallowed the egg. The coyote started to run. The prince said "God and Lion," and turned into a lion and gave chase. The coyote then turned into a hare, which hid in the underbrush where the lion was unable to follow it.

The prince said "God and Hound," became a hound and began to chase the hare. The hare, finding itself in danger of being captured, quickly changed itself back into a pigeon. The eagle caught the pigeon, flew to earth with the dead pigeon in its claws, opened up the dead bird and with a single blow of its beak broke the egg. Then instead of a dead pigeon there was a dead giant in its place.

The eagle flew back to the castle and entered the maiden's bedroom. There he said "God and Man," assumed his human form, and took into his arms the beautiful maiden. Forgetting their fear of the giant, they were married and changed the gloomy castle into a nest of love and happiness.

Source: "The Giant's Secret," Gabriel A. Cordova Jr. "Magic Tales of Mexico," M.A. Thesis. Texas Western College, El Paso, TX, 1951. http://www.genecowan.com/magictales/, retrieved August 6, 2008.

La Llorona

The legend of La Llorona (Spanish, "the weeping woman") is perhaps the best known and most widely distributed Mexican folktale in North America. Commentators commonly note that La Llorona is a composite character drawing on features of Cihuacoatl (an Aztec female deity associated with both death and childbirth), La Malinche (the Native American woman who served as Cortez' interpreter and, according to folk legend, his mistress), and the heroines of various folktales of poor women jilted by high-born men whose rejection leads to infanticide. In many communities, La Llorona is often used as a bogey figure to frighten disobedient children.

As is generally known, many bad things are met with by night in the streets of the city; but this Wailing Woman, *La Llorona*, is the very worst of them all. She is worse by far than the *vaca de lumbre* that at midnight comes forth from the *potrero* of San Pablo and goes galloping through the streets like a blazing whirlwind, breathing forth from her nostrils smoke and sparks and flames: because the Fiery Cow, Senor, while a dangerous animal to look at, really does no harm whatever and La Llorona is as harmful as she can be!

Seeing her walking quietly along the quiet street at the times when she is not running, and shrieking for her lost children she seems a respectable person, only odd looking because of her white petticoat and the white *reboso* with which her head is covered, and anybody might speak to her. But whoever does speak to her, in that very same moment dies!

The beginning of her was so long ago that no one knows when was the beginning of her; nor does any one know anything about her at all. But it is known certainly that at the beginning of her, when she was a living woman, she committed bad sins. As soon as ever a child was born to her she would throw it into one of the canals which surround the City, and so would drown it; and she had a great many children, and this practice in regard to them she continued for a long time. At last her conscience began to prick her about what she did with her children; but whether it was that the priest spoke to her, or that some of the saints cautioned her in the matter, no one knows. But it is certain that because of her sinnings she began to go through the streets in the darkness weeping and wailing. And presently it was said that from night till morning there was a wailing woman in the streets; and to see her, being in terror of her, many people went forth at midnight; but none did see her, because she could be seen only when the street was deserted and she was alone.

Sometimes she would come to a sleeping watchman, and would waken him by asking: "What time is it?" And he would see a woman clad in white standing beside him with her reboso drawn over her face. And he would answer: "It is twelve hours of the night." And she would say: "At twelve hours of this day I must be in Guadalajara!" or it might be in San Luis Potosi, or in some other far distant city and, so speaking, she would shriek bitterly: "Where shall I find my children?" and would vanish instantly and utterly away. And the watchman would feel as though all his senses had gone from him, and would become as a dead man. This happened many times to many watchmen, who made report of it to their officers; but their officers would not believe what they told. But it happened, on a night, that an officer of the watch was passing by the lonely street beside the church of Santa Anita. And there he met with a woman wearing a white reboso and a white petticoat; and to her he began to make love. He urged her, saying: "Throw off your reboso that I may see your pretty face!"

And suddenly she uncovered her face and what he beheld was a bare grinning skull set fast to the bare bones of a skeleton! And while he looked at her, being in horror, there came from her fleshless jaws an icy breath; and the iciness of it froze the very heart's blood in him, and he fell to the earth heavily in a deathly swoon. When his senses came back to him he was greatly troubled. In fear he returned to the Diputacion, and there told what had befallen him. And in a little while his life forsook him and he died.

What is most wonderful about this Wailing Woman is that she is seen in the same moment by different people in places widely apart: one seeing her hurrying across the atrium of the Cathedral; another beside the Arcos de San Cosme; and yet another near the Salto del Agua, over by the prison of Belen. More than that, in one single night she will be seen in Monterey and in Oaxaca and in Acapulco the whole width and length of the land apart and whoever speaks with her in those far cities, as here in Mexico, immediately dies in fright. Also, she is seen at times in the country.

Once some travellers coming along a lonely road met with her, and asked: "Where go you on this lonely road?"

And for answer she cried: "Where shall I find my children?" and, shrieking, disappeared. And one of the travellers went mad. Being come here to the City they told what they had seen; and were told that this same Wailing Woman had maddened or killed many people here also.

Because the Wailing Woman is so generally known and so greatly feared, few people now stop her when they meet with her to speak with her therefore few now die of her, and that is fortunate. But her loud keen wailings, and the sound of her running feet, are heard often; and especially in nights of storm. I myself, Senor, have heard the running of her feet and her wailings; but I never have seen her. God forbid that I ever shall!

Source: "The Legend of La Llorona," Thomas A. Janvier, *The Legends of the City of Mexico* (New York: Harper & Brothers, 1910), pp. 134–138.

Bullet-Swallower

In the following personal experience narrative of an encounter with the supernatural, Traga-Balas (Bullet-Swallower) substantiates the power of his Catholic beliefs by embedding his tale of an animate corpse in accounts of his physically harrowing life.

He was a wiry little man, a bundle of nerves in perpetual motion. Quicksilver might have run through his veins instead of blood. His right arm, partly paralyzed as result of a machete cut he had received in a saloon brawl, terminated in stiff, claw-like, dirty-nailed fingers. One eye was partly closed—a knife cut had done that—but the other, amber in color, had the alertness and the quickness of a hawk's. Chairs were not made for him. Squatting on the floor or sitting on one heel, he told interminable stories of border feuds, bandit raids and smuggler fights as he fingered a curved, murderous knife which ended in three inches of zigzag, jagged steel. "No one has ever escaped this," he would say, caressing it. "Sticking it into a man might not have finished him, but getting it out—ah, my friend, that did the work. It's a very old one, brought from Spain, I guess," he would add in an unconcerned voice. "Here is the date, 1630."

A landowner by inheritance, a trail driver by necessity, and a smuggler and gambler by choice, he had given up the traditions of his family to be and do that which pleased him most. Through some freakish mistake he had been born three centuries too late. He might have been a fearless conquistador, or he might have been a chivalrous knight of the Rodrigo de Narváez type, fighting the infidels along the Moorish frontier. A tireless horseman, a man of *pelo en pecho* (hair on the chest), as he braggingly called himself, he was afraid of nothing.

"The men of my time were not lily-livered, white-gizzarded creatures," he would boast. "We fought for the thrill of it, and the sight of blood maddened us as it does a bull. Did we receive a gash on the stomach? Did the guts come out? What of it? We tightened our sash and continued the fray. See this arm? Ah, could it but talk, it could tell you how many men it sent to the other world. To Hell perhaps, perhaps to Purgatory, but none I am sure to Heaven. The men I associated with were neither sissies nor saints. Often at night when I can not sleep because of the pain in these cursed wounds, I say a prayer, in my way, for their souls, in case my prayers should reach the good God."

"People call me Traga-Balas, Bullet-Swallower—Antonio Traga-Balas, to be more exact. Ay, were I as young as I was when the incident that gave me this name happened!"

"We were bringing several cart loads of smuggled goods to be delivered at once and in safety to the owner. Oh, no, the freight was not ours but we would have fought for it with our life's blood. We had dodged the Mexican officials, and now we had to deal with the Texas Rangers. They must have been tipped, because they knew the exact hour we were to cross the river. We swam in safety. The pack mules, loaded with packages wrapped in tanned hides, we led by the bridle. We hid the mules in a clump of tules [reeds] and were just beginning to dress when the Rangers fell upon us. Of course, we did not have a stitch of clothes on; did you think we swam fully dressed? Had we but had our guns in readiness, there might have been a different story to tell. We would have fought like wildcats to keep the smuggled goods from falling into their hands. It was not ethical among smugglers to lose the property of a Mexican to Americans, and as to falling ourselves into their hands, we preferred death a thousand times. It's no disgrace and dishonor to die like a man, but it is to die like a rat. Only canaries sing; men never tell, however tortured they may be. I have seen the Rangers pumping water into the mouth of an innocent man because he would not confess to something he had not done. But that is another story."

"I ran to where the pack mules were to get my gun. Like a fool that I was, I kept yelling at the top of my voice, 'You so, and so gringo [derogatory term for Anglo-Americans] cowards, why don't you attack men like men? Why do you wait until they are undressed and unarmed?' I must have said some very insulting things, for one of them shot at me right in the mouth. The bullet knocked all of my front teeth out, grazed my tongue and went right through the back of my neck. Didn't kill me, though. It takes more than bullets to kill Antonio Traga-Balas."

"The next thing I knew I found myself in a shepherd's hut. I had been left for dead, no doubt, and I had been found by the goatherd. The others were sent to the penitentiary. After I recovered, I remained in hiding for a year or so; and when I showed myself all thought it a miracle that I had lived through. That's how I was rechristened Traga-Balas. That confounded bullet did leave my neck a little stiff; I can't turn around as easily as I should, but outside of that I am as fit as though the accident—I like to call it that—had never happened. It takes a lot to kill a man, at least one who can swallow bullets."

"I've seen and done many strange things in my life and I can truthfully say that I have never been afraid but once. 'What are bullets and knife thrusts to seeing a corpse arise from its coffin? Bullets can be dodged and dagger cuts are harmless unless they hit a vital spot. But a dead man staring with lifeless, open eyes and gaping mouth is enough to make a man tremble in his boots. And, mind you, I am not a coward, never have been. Is there any one among you who thinks Antonio Traga-Balas is a coward?"

At a question like this, Traga-Balas would take the knife from its cover and finger it in a way that gave one a queer, empty spot in the stomach. Now he was launched upon a story.

"This thing happened," he went on, "years ago at Roma beside the Rio Bravo [Rio Grande River]. I was at home alone; my wife and children were visiting in another town. I remember it was a windy night in November. The evening was cool, and, not knowing what else to do, I decided to go to bed early. I was not asleep yet when someone began pounding at my door. 'Open the door, Don Antonio; please let me in,' said a woman's voice. I got up and recognized in the woman before me one of our new neighbors. They had just moved into a deserted jacal in the alley back of our house. 'My husband is very sick,' she explained. 'He is dying and wants to see you. He says he must speak to you before he dies.' "

"I dressed and went out with her, wondering all the time what this unknown man wanted to see me about. I found him in a miserable hovel, on a more miserable pallet on the floor, and I could see by his sunken cheeks and the fire that burned in his eyes that he was really dying, and of consumption, too. With mumbled words he dismissed the woman from the room and, once she had gone, he asked me to help him sit up. I propped him on the pillows the best I could. He was seized with a fit of coughing followed by a hemorrhage and I was almost sure that he would die before he could say anything. I brought him some water and poured a little tequila from a half empty bottle that was at the head of the pallet. After drinking it, he gave a sigh of relief. 'I am much better now,' he whispered. His voice was already failing. 'My friend,' he went on, 'excuse my calling you, an utter stranger, but I have heard you are a man of courage and of honor and you will understand what I have to say to you. That woman you saw here is really not my wife; but I have lived with her in sin for the last twenty years. It weighs upon my conscience and I want to right the wrong I did her once.' "

"As the man ended this confession, I could not help thinking what changes are brought about in the soul by the mere thought of facing eternity. I thought it very strange that after so long a time he should have qualms of conscience now. Yet I imagine death is a fearful thing, and, never having died myself nor been afraid to die, I could not judge what the dying man before me was feeling. So I decided to do what I would have expected others to do for me, and asked him if there was anything I might do for him."

" 'Call a priest. I want to marry her,' he whispered."

"I did as he commanded and went to the rectory. Father José Maria was still saying his prayers, and when I told him that I had come to get him to marry a dying man, he looked at me in a way he had of doing whenever he doubted anyone, with one eye half closed and out of the corner of the other.

As I had played him many pranks in the past, no doubt he thought I was now playing another. He hesitated at first but then got up somewhat convinced.''

'' 'I'll take my chance with you again, you son of Barabbas [one of the thieves who was to be executed with Christ, but who was freed by vote of the mob],' he said. 'I'll go. Some poor soul may want to reconcile himself with his Creator.' He put on his black cape and took the little bag he always carried on such occasions. The night was as black as the mouth of a wolf and the wind was getting colder and stronger.''

'' 'A bad time for anyone to want a priest, eh, Father?' I said in an effort to make conversation, not knowing what else to say.''

'' 'The hour of repentance is a blessed moment at whatever time it comes,' he replied in a tone that I thought was reprimanding.''

"On entering the house, we found the man alone. The woman was in the kitchen, he told us. I joined her there, and what do you suppose the shameless creature was doing? Drinking tequila, getting courage, she told me, for the ordeal ahead of her. After about an hour, we were called into the sick room. The man looked much better. Unburdening his soul had given him that peaceful look you sometimes see on the face of the dead who die while smiling. I was told that I was to be witness to the Holy Sacrament of Matrimony. The woman was so drunk by now she could hardly stand up; and between hiccoughs she promised to honor and love the man who was more fit to be food for the worms than for life in this valley of tears. I'd never seen a man so strong for receiving sacraments as that one was. He had received the Sacrament of Penance, then that of Matrimony—and I could see no greater penance than marrying such a woman—and now he was to receive Extreme Unction, the Sacrament for the Dying.''

"The drunken woman and I held candles as Father José Maria anointed him with holy oil; and when we had to join him in prayer, I was ashamed that I could not repeat even the Lord's Prayer with him. That scene will always live in my mind, and when I die may I have as holy a man as Father José Maria to pray for me! He lingered a few moments; then, seeing there was nothing else to do, he said he would go back. I went with him under the pretext of getting something or other for the dying man, but in reality I wanted to see him safe at home. On the way back to the dying man I stopped at the saloon for another bottle of tequila. The dying man might need a few drops to give him courage to start on his journey to the Unknown, although from what I had seen I judged that Father José Maria had given him all he needed.''

"When I returned, the death agony was upon him. The drunken woman was snoring in the kitchen. It was my responsibility to see that the man did not die like a dog. I wet his cracked lips with a piece of cloth moistened in tequila. I watched all night. The howling of the wind and the death rattle of the consumptive made the place the devil's kingdom. With the coming of dawn, the man's soul, now pure from sin, left the miserable carcass that had given it lodging during life. I folded his arms over his chest and covered his face with a cloth. There was no use in calling the woman; she lay on the dirt floor of the kitchen snoring like a trumpet. I closed the door and went out to see what could be done about arrangements for the funeral. I went home and got a little money—I did not have much—to buy some boards for the coffin, black calico for the covering and for a mourning dress for the bride, now a widow—although I felt she did not deserve it—and candles."

"I made the coffin, and when all was done and finished went back to the house. The woman was still snoring, her half-opened mouth filled with buzzing flies. The corpse was as I had left it. I called some of the neighbors to help me dress the dead man in my one black suit, but he was stiff already and we had to lay him in the coffin as he was, unwashed and dirty. If it is true that we wear white raiments in Heaven, I hope the good San Pedro gave him one at the entrance before the other blessed spirits got to see the pitiful things he wore. I watched the body all day; he was to be buried early the following morning. Father José Maria had told me he would say Mass for him. The old woman, curse her, had gotten hold of the other bottle of tequila and continued bottling up courage for the ordeal that she said she had to go through."

"The wind that had started the night before did not let down; in fact, it was getting stronger. Several times the candles had blown out, and the corpse and I had been left in utter darkness. To avoid the repetition of such a thing, I went to the kitchen and got some empty fruit cans very much prized by the old woman. In truth, she did not want to let me use them at first, because, she said, the fruit on the paper wrapping looked so natural and was the only fruit she had ever owned. I got them anyway, filled them with corn, and stuck the candles there."

"Early in the evening about nine, or thereabouts, I decided to get out again and ask some people to come and watch with me part of the night. Not that I was afraid to stay alone with the corpse. One might fear the spirits of those who die in sin, but certainly not this one who had left the world the way a Christian should leave it. I left somewhat regretfully, for I was beginning to have a kindly feeling towards the dead man. I felt towards that body as I would feel towards a friend, no doubt because I had helped it to transform itself from a human being to a nice Christian corpse."

"As I went from house to house asking people to watch with me that night, I was reminded of a story that the priest had told us once, and by the time I had gone half through the town I knew very well how the man who was inviting guests to the wedding feast must have felt. All had some good excuse to give but no one could come. To make a long story short, I returned alone, to spend the last watch with my friend the corpse."

"As I neared the house, I saw it was very well lighted, and I thought perhaps some people had finally taken pity upon the poor unfortunate and had gone there with more candles to light the place. But soon I realized what was really happening. The jacal was on fire."

"I ran inside. The sight that met my eyes was one I shall ever see. I was nailed to the floor with terror. The corpse, its hair a flaming mass, was sitting up in the coffin where it had so peacefully lain all day. Its glassy, opaque eyes stared into space with a look that saw nothing and its mouth was convulsed into the most horrible grin. I stood there paralyzed by the horror of the scene. To make matters worse, the drunken woman reeled into the room, yelling 'He is burning before he gets to Hell!' "

"Two thoughts ran simultaneously through my mind: to get her out of the room and to extinguish the fire. I pushed the screaming woman out into the darkness and, arming myself with courage, reentered the room. I was wearing cowboy boots, and my feet were the only part of my body well protected. Closing my eyes, I kicked the table, and I heard the thud of the burning body as it hit the floor. I became crazy then. With my booted feet I tramped upon and kicked the corpse until I thought the fire was extinguished. I dared not open my eyes for fear of what I might see, and with my eyes still closed I ran out of the house. I did not stop until I reached the rectory. Like mad I pounded upon the door, and when the priest opened it and saw me standing there looking more like a ghost than a living person, he could but cross himself. It was only after I had taken a drink or two—may God forgive me for having done so in his presence—that I could tell him what had happened."

"He went back with me and, with eyes still closed, I helped him place the poor dead man in his coffin. Father José Maria prayed all night. As for me, I sat staring at the wall, not daring once to look at the coffin, much less upon the charred corpse. That was the longest watch I ever kept."

"At five o'clock, with no one to help us, we carried the coffin to the church, where the promised mass was said. We hired a burro cart to take the dead man to the cemetery, and, as the sun was coming up, Father José Maria, that man of God, and I, an unpenitent sinner, laid him in his final resting place."

Source: "Bullet Swallower," Jovita Gonzalez. *Puro Mexicano*, J. Frank Dobie, ed. *Publications of the Texas Folklore Society*, no. 12 (Austin: Texas Folk-Lore Society, 1935), pp. 107–114.

The Accursed Bell

The legend of "The Accursed Bell" illustrates the continuity of European beliefs in the supernatural into the New World context. At its center is the concept of the extraordinary and real power of the Devil that propelled the Spanish Inquisition. Animosity against Moors, heretics, and the French, whose intervention in Mexican affairs made possible the brief reign of Emperor Maximillian (1864–1867) of Mexico, are apparent in the narrative as well

This story, *Señor*, is about the accursed bell that once was the clock-bell of the Palace. It has so many beginnings that the only way really to get at the bones of it would be for a number of people, all talking at once, to tell the different first parts of it at the same time. For, you see, the curse that was upon this bell that caused it to be brought to trial before the *Consejo* of the Inquisition, and by the *Consejo* to be condemned to have its wicked tongue torn out and to be banished from Spain to this country was made up of several curses which had been in use in other ways elsewhere previously: so that one beginning is with the Moor, and another with Don Gil de Marcadante, and another with the devil-forged armor, and still another with the loosing of all the curses from the cross (wherein for some hundreds of years they were imprisoned) and the fusing of them into the one great curse wherewith this unfortunate bell was afflicted which happened when that holy emblem was refounded, and with the metal of it this bell was made.

Concerning the Moor, *Señor*, I can give you very little information. All that I know about him is that he had the bad name of Muslef; and that he was killed as he deserved to be killed, being an Infidel, by a Christian knight; and that this knight cut his head off and brought it home with him as an agreeable memento of the occasion, and was very pleased with what he had done. Unfortunately, this knight also brought home with him the Moor's armor which was of bronze, and so curiously and so beautifully wrought that it evidently had been forged by devils, and which was farther charged with devilishness because it had been worn by an Infidel; and then, still more unfortunately, he neglected to have the armor purified by causing the devils to be exorcised out of it by a Christian priest. Therefore, of course, the devils remained in the armor ready to make trouble whenever they got the chance.

How Don Gil de Marcadante came to be the owner of that accursed devil-possessed armor, *Señor,* I never have heard mentioned. Perhaps he bought it because it happened to fit him; and, certainly he being a most unusually sinful young gentleman the curse that was upon it and the devils which were a part of it fitted him to a hair.

This Don Gil was a student of law in Toledo; but his studies were the very last things to which he turned his attention, and the life that he led was the shame of his respectable brother and his excellent mother's despair. Habitually, he broke every law of the Decalogue, and so brazenly that all the city rang with the stories of his evil doings and his crimes. Moreover, he was of a blusterous nature and a born brawler: ready at the slightest contradiction to burst forth with such a torrent of blasphemies and imprecations that his mouth seemed to be a den of snakes and toads and scorpions; and ever quick to snatch his sword out and to get on in a hurry from words to blows. As his nearest approach to good nature was after he had killed someone in a quarrel of his own making, and as even at those favorable times his temper was of a brittleness, he was not looked upon as an agreeable companion and had few friends.

This Don Gil had most intimate relations with the devil, as was proved in various ways. Thus, a wound that he received in one of his duels instantly closed and healed itself; on a night of impenetrable darkness, as he went about his evil doings, he was seen to draw apart the heavy gratings of a window as though the thick iron bars had been silken threads; and a stone that he cast at a man in one of his rages mercifully not hitting him remained burning hot in the place where it had fallen for several days. Moreover, it was known generally that in the night time, in a very secret and hidden part of his dwelling, he gave himself up to hideous and most horrible sacrileges in which his master the devil had always a part. And so these facts and others of a like nature coming to the knowledge of the Holy Office, it was perceived that he was a sorcerer. Therefore he was marched off wearing his devil-forged armor, to which fresh curses had come with his use of it to a cell in the Inquisition; and to make sure of holding him fast until the next *auto de fe* came round, when he was to be burned properly and regularly, he was bound with a great chain, and the chain was secured firmly to a strong staple in the cell wall.

But the devil, *Señor,* sometimes saves his own. On a morning, the jailer went as usual to Don Gil's cell with the bread and the water for him; and when he had opened the cell door he saw, as he believed, Don Gil in his armor waiting as usual for his bread and his water; but in a moment he perceived that what he saw was not Don Gil in his armor, but only the accursed armor standing upright full of emptiness; and that the staple was torn out; and that the great chain was broken; and that Don Gil was gone!

And then so much to the horror of the jailer that he immediately went mad of it the empty armor began slowly to walk up and down the cell!

After that time Don Gil never was seen, nor was he heard of, again on earth; and so on earth, when the time came for burning him at the *auto de fe* [Spanish, "declaration of faith," euphemism for burning at the stake], he had to be burned in effigy. However, as there could be no doubt about the place to which the devil had taken him everybody was well satisfied that he got his proper personal burning elsewhere.

Then it was, *Señor,* that the Holy Office most wisely ordered that that devil-possessed and doubly accursed armor should be melted, and refounded into a cross: knowing that the sanctity of that blessed emblem would quiet the curses and would hold the devils still and fast. Therefore that order was executed; and the wisdom of it which some had questioned, on the ground that devils and curses were unsuitable material to make a cross of was apparent as soon as the bronze turned fluid in the furnace: because there came from the fiery seething midst of it to the dazed terror of the workmen shouts of devil-laughter, and imprecations horrible to listen to, and frightful blasphemies; and to these succeeded, as the metal was being poured into the mould, a wild outburst of defiant remonstrance; and then all this demoniac fury died away as the metal hardened and became fixed as a cross at first into half-choked cries of agony, and then into confused lamentations, and at the last into little whimpering moans. Thus the devils and the curses were disposed of: and then the cross holding them imprisoned in its holy substance was set up in a little townlet not far from Madrid in which just then a cross happened to be wanted; and there it remained usefully for some hundreds of years.

At the end of that period by which time everybody was dead who knew what was inside of it, the cross was asked for by the Priory of a little convent in that townlet near Madrid, who desired it that he might have it refounded into a bell; and as the Prior was a worthy person, and as he really needed a bell, his request was granted. So they made out of the cross a very beautiful bell: having on one side of it the two-headed eagle; and having on the other side of it a calvario; and having at the top of it, for its hanging, two imperial lions supporting a cross-bar in the shape of a crown. Then it was hung in the tower of the little convent; and the Prior, and all the Brothers with him, were very much pleased. But that worthy Prior, and those equally worthy Brothers, were not pleased for long, because the curses and the devils all were loose again and their chance to do new wickednesses had come!

On a night of blackness, without any warning whatever, the whole of the townlet was awakened by the prodigious clangor of a bell furiously ringing. In an instant seeking the cause of this disturbance everybody came out into the night's blackness: the *Señor Cura* [priest], the *Señor Alcalde* [mayor], the *alguaciles* [bailiffs], the Prior, the Brothers, all the townsfolk to the very last one.

And when they had looked about them they found that the cause of the disturbance was the new bell of the convent, which was ringing with such an excessive violence that the night's blackness was corrupted with its noise.

Terror was upon everyone; and greater terror was upon everyone when it was found out that the door of the bell-tower was locked, and that the bell was ringing of its lone self: because the bad fact then became evident that only devils could have the matter in hand. The Alcalde alone being a very valiant gentleman, and not much believing in devils was not satisfied with that ringing. Therefore the Alcalde caused the door to be unlocked and, carrying a torch with him, entered the bell-tower; and there he found the bell-rope crazily flying up and down as though a dozen men were pulling it, and nobody was pulling it, which sight somewhat shook his nerves.

However, because of his valorousness, he only stopped to cross himself; and then he went on bravely up the belfry stair. But what he saw when he was come into the belfry fairly brought him to a stand. For there was the bell ringing tempestuously; and never a visible hand was near it; and the only living thing that he found in the belfry was a great black cat with its tail bushed out and its fur bristling which evil animal for a moment leered at him malignantly, with its green eyes gleaming in the torchlight, and then sprang past him and dashed down the stair.

Then the *Señor Alcalde,* no longer doubting that the bell was being rung by devils, and himself not knowing how to manage devils, called down from the belfry to the *Señor Cura* to come up and take charge of the matter, whereupon the *Señor Cura,* holding his courage in both hands, did come up into the belfry, bringing his *hisopo* [hyssop; instrument for sprinkling holy water] with him, and fell to sprinkling the bell with holy water which seemed to him, so far as he could see his way into that difficult tangle, the best thing that he could do. But his doing it, of course, was the very worst thing that he could have done: because, you see, Senor, the devils were angered beyond all endurance by being scalded with the holy water (that being the effect that holy water has upon devils) and so only rang the bell the more furiously in their agony of pain. Then the *Señor Alcalde* and the *Señor Cura* perceived that they could not quiet the devils, and decided to give up trying to. Therefore they came down from the belfry together and they, and everybody with them, went away through the night's blackness crossing themselves, and were glad to be safe again in their homes.

The next day the *Señor Alcalde* made a formal inquest into the whole matter: citing to appear before him all the townsfolk and all the Brothers, and questioning them closely every one. And the result of this inquest was to make certain that the bell-ringer of the convent had not rung the bell; nor had any other of the Brothers rung it; nor had any of the townsfolk rung it. Therefore the *Señor Alcalde,* and with him the *Señor Cura* whose opinion was of importance in such a matter decided that the devil had rung it: and their decision was accepted by everybody, because that was what everybody from the beginning had believed.

Therefore because such devilish doings affected the welfare of the whole kingdom a formal report of all that had happened was submitted to the Cortes; and the Cortes, after pondering the report seriously, perceived that the matter was ecclesiastical and referred it to the Consejo of the Inquisition; and the members of the Consejo, in due course, ordered that all the facts should be digested and regularized and an opinion passed upon them by their Fiscal.

Being a very painstaking person, the Fiscal went at his work with so great an earnestness that for more than a year he was engaged upon it. First he read all that he could find to read about bells in all the Spanish law books, from the Siete Partidas of Alonzo the Wise downward; then he read all that he could find about bells in such law books of foreign countries as were accessible to him; then, in the light of the information so obtained, he digested and regularized the facts of the case presented for his consideration and applied himself to writing his opinion upon them; and then, at last, he came before the Consejo and read to that body his opinion from beginning to end. Through the whole of a long day the Fiscal read his opinion; and through the whole of the next day, and the next, and the next; and at the end of the fourth day he finished the reading of his opinion and sat down. And the opinion of the Fiscal was that the devil had rung the bell.

Then the Consejo, after debating for three days upon what had been read by the Fiscal, gave formal approval to his opinion; and in conformity with it the Consejo came to these conclusions:

1. That the ringing of the bell was a matter of no importance to good Christians.
2. That the bell, being possessed of a devil, should have its tongue torn out: so that never again should it dare to ring of its lone devilish self, to the peril of human souls.
3. That the bell, being dangerous to good Christians, should be banished from the Spanish Kingdom to the Indies, and forever should remain tongueless and exiled overseas.

Thereupon, that wise sentence was executed. The devil-possessed bell was taken down from the belfry of the little convent, and its wicked tongue was torn out of it; then it was carried shamefully and with insults to the coast; then it was put on board of one of the ships of the float bound for Mexico; and in Mexico, in due course, it arrived. Being come here, and no orders coming with it regarding its disposition, it was brought from Vera Cruz to the Capital and was placed in an odd corner of one of the corridors of the Palace: and there it remained quietly everybody being shy of meddling with a bell that was known to be alive with witchcraft for some hundreds of years.

In that same corner it still was, Senor, when the Conde de Revillagigedo only a little more than a century ago became Viceroy; and as soon as that most energetic gentleman saw it he wanted to know in a hurry being indisposed to let anything or anybody rust in idleness why a bell that needed only a tongue in it to make it serviceable was not usefully employed. For some time no one could tell him anything more about the bell than that there was a curse upon it; and that answer did not satisfy him, because curses did not count for much in his very practical mind. In the end a very old clerk in the Secretariat gave him the bell's true story; and proved the truth of it by bringing out from deep in the archives an ancient yellowed parchment: which was precisely the royal order, following the decree of the Consejo, that the bell should have its tongue torn out, and forever should remain tongueless and exiled overseas.

With that order before him, even the Conde de Revillagigedo, Senor, did not venture to have a new tongue put into the bell and to set it to regular work again; but what he did do came to much the same thing. At that very time he was engaged in pushing to a brisk completion the repairs to the Palace that had gone on for a hundred years languishingly, following the burning of it in the time of the Viceroy Don Gaspar de la Cerda and among his repairings was the replacement of the Palace clock. Now a clock-bell, Senor, does not need a tongue in it, being struck with hammers from the outside; and so the Conde, whose wits were of an alertness, perceived in a moment that by employing the bell as a clock-bell he could make it useful again without traversing the king's command. And that was what immediately he did with it and that was how the Palace clock came to have foisted upon it this accursed bell.

But, so far as I have heard, Senor, this bell conducted itself as a clock-bell with a perfect regularity and propriety: probably because the devils which were in it had grown too old to be dangerously hurtful, and because the curse that was upon it had weakened with time. I myself, as a boy and as a young man, have heard it doing its duty always punctually, and no doubt it still would be doing its duty had not the busybodying French seen fit during the period of the Intervention, when they meddled with everything to put another bell in the place of it and to have it melted down. What was done with the metal when the bell was melted, Senor, I do not know; but I have been told by an old founder of my acquaintance that nothing was done with it: because, as he very positively assured me, when the bell was melted the metal of it went sour in the furnace and refused to be recast.

If that is true, Senor, it looks as though all those devils in the bell which came to it from the Moor and from the devil-forged armor and from Don Gil de Marcadante still had some strength for wickedness left to them even in their old age.

Source: "The Legend of the Accursed Bell," Thomas A. Janvier. *The Legends of the City of Mexico* (New York: Harper & Brothers, 1910), pp. 69–83.

El Señor Milagroso Rescues
a Stingy Son

A widely distributed feature of Latino folk Catholicism is directing one's appeals for divine help through saints' images—santitos. In many cases, tokens of an appeal or of an answered prayer are placed with the santito. These images, frequently labeled milagros (literally, "miracles"), are usually caste from gold or silver and are representations of the limb (an arm or leg, for example) or organ (e.g., a heart) healed or, as in the case described in the following legend, a physical depiction of an extraordinary event.

El Señor Milagroso ("the Miraculous Lord"), the miracle worker, is an image treasured as one of the most valued religious possessions of Matanzas [Cuba]. Although the church has offered many thousands of dollars for its possession, and its owner is in comparatively poor circumstances, it still remains in the hands of a private family.

It has been handed down through many generations of the Castro family and is at present in the possession of Señor Arturo Castro who has built a shrine where all are welcome to visit and revere the saint.

This saint is supposed to instantly answer the prayer of those who are in great danger. A curious story is connected with the image of a snake twined about the body of a man that is placed before in the saint.

During the revolution of 1868 when many well-to-do families were temporarily reduced to needy circumstances an old man was accustomed to visit his married son about the time of the midday meal. The son, who found it difficult to fill the all too many mouths of his own household, one day ordered the meal to be kept back until his father had gone. The father came and, failing to see the usual preparations for breakfast in progress, inquired if the meal had already been served. He was given to understand that it had and left the house somewhat nettled, as was natural.

The dish was now ordered to be placed on the table with the least possible delay. As moments passed and no food appeared, the master of the house went to the kitchen to inquire the causes of delay and there found the servant struggling to lift the cover from a kettle. Angry at the inability to perform so apparently simple a task, he gave the cover a pull and then slowly from the boiling liquid appeared the shining coils of a monstrous serpent, which wound itself about the body of the selfish son! Imagine the confusion and consternation in which the household was thrown on seeing their master in the coils of this huge monster.

The master, finding it impossible to release himself from the coils of the serpent and realizing that this was the punishment of God for deceiving his parent, vowed to present the Señor Milagroso a silver image of the incident if he was released safely. He was freed from the serpent's coils and soon after had the image made that rests at the feet of the saint's image.

Source: "Superstition and Witchcraft in Cuba," L. Roy Terwilliger. *Cuban Folk-Lore* (Havana: Avisador Comercial Printing House, 1908), p. 18.

The Penitent Brothers

The following account of an encounter with the Penitentes, a folk religious order of New Mexico, utilizes the traditional personal experience narrative as a literary frame. In addition, embedded within this account are folk beliefs maintained by the group in the late nineteenth century (such as beliefs in witchcraft and the power of Satan), additional local narratives (such as Manuel Martin's encounter with the ghost Penitentes), and additional background on regional heroes (such as Colonel Manuel Chaves mentioned elsewhere in this volume; see "A New Mexico David").

"Until recent times the practice of self-flagellation as a religious custom continued to manifest itself intermittently in the south of France, and also in Italy and Spain; and so late as 1820 a procession of flagellants took place at Lisbon." So the *Encyclopaedia Britannica* winds up what is intended to be a complete outline of the history of self-whipping as a means of grace.

Aye, verily! And so late as 1891 a procession of flagellants took place within the limits of the United States. A procession in which voters of this Republic shredded their naked backs with savage whips, staggered beneath huge crosses, and hugged the maddening needles of the cactus; a procession which culminated in the flesh-and-blood crucifixion of an unworthy representative of the Redeemer. Nor was this an isolated horror. Every Good Friday, for many generations, it has been a staple custom to hold these rites in parts of New Mexico.

The order of Los Hermanos Penitentes (the Penitent Brothers) was founded in Spain some 300 years ago. It had nothing of the scourge in its original plan. Its members met for religious study and conversation, and were men of good morals and good sense "according to their lights." The seeds of the order were brought to Mexico, and later to what is now New Mexico, by the Franciscan friars with the Spanish Conquistadores.

Lent is the sole season of Penitente activity. The rest of the year their religion is allowed to lapse in desuetude more or less innocuous, and the brethren placidly follow their various vocations as laborers, cowboys, or shepherds. With the beginning of the sacred forty days, however, they enter upon the convenient task of achieving their piety for the year.

Every Friday night in Lent the belated wayfarer among the interior ranges is liable to be startled by the hideous "too-ootle-te-too" of an unearthly whistle which wails over and over its refrain. As the midnight wind sweeps that weird strain down the lonely canon, it seems the wail of a lost spirit. I have known men of tried bravery to flee from that sound when they heard it for the first time.

The hamlet of San Mateo a straggling procession of brown adobes at the very foot of the mesa foundation of Mount Taylor, at an altitude of nearly eight thousand feet contains four hundred people. It is perhaps the most unreclaimed Mexican village in New Mexico. Not half a dozen of its people speak English. In 1887, a witch was stoned to death there, who had played the cynical trick of turning an estimable citizen into a woman for the space of three months! Numerous other inhabitants have suffered though none else so severely at the hands of witches, and several in the town have seen and held converse with his Satanic Majesty! Little wonder, then, that the dwindling Penitentes have still kept a foothold there, or that the population is in awed and active sympathy with their brutalities.

I had been watching feverishly for Holy Week to come. No photographer had ever caught the Penitentes with his sun-lasso [i.e., camera], and I was assured of death in various unattractive forms at the first hint of an attempt. But when the ululation filled the ear at night, enthusiasm crowded prudence to the wall. The village air grew heavy with mysterious whisperings and solemn expectancy. Whatever they talked about, the people were evidently thinking of nothing else. I wandered through fields and arroyos at all hours of night, trying to trail that mysterious whistle whose echoes seemed to come from all points of the compass; but in vain. My utmost reward was a glimpse of three ghostly figures just disappearing inside Juanito's house on the hill.

But at last March 20th came around, and with it Holy Thursday. At 9:00 AM the shrilling of the pito close at hand called us out of the house in haste, but already the three responsible Penitentes had vanished in the tall chaparral. We greased the rattling buckboard, and hurried over to the village. Everyone was out, but they were no longer the friendly *paisanos* we had known. The sight of the camera-box and tripod provoked ominous scowls and mutterings on every hand. Nine-tenths of the population were clustered in close, listless groups along a little wart of houses upon a hill which overhangs the *camposanto* (burying-ground), at the upper end of town.

Squatting with backs against the 'dobe walls, the men rolled cigarettes from corn-husks or brown paper, and talked intermittently. The women nursed their babes unconstrainedly, and rolled brown-paper or corn-husk cigarettes. I stowed the obnoxious instrument inside a friendly house, and waited. Waiting seems natural in a Mexican town. The minutes loafed into hours, and still the talking, the nursing, the smoking went on. Nobody thought of moving.

It was 2:00 PM when a stir in the crowd on the hilltop told us that it was coming at last, and the camera was straightway planted behind the adobe ramparts of the door yard. In five minutes more a fifer came over the ridge, followed by five women singing hymns, and behind them a half-naked figure with bagged head, swinging his deliberate whip, whose swish, thud! swish, thud! we could hear plainly two hundred yards away, punctuating the weird music. In measured step the pilgrims paced along the reeling footpath, and disappeared around a spur toward the morada. Half an hour later the fife again asserted itself up the canyon, and soon reappeared with its persecutor, the singing women and the lone self-torturer. As he passed on to the grave-yard, we saw that little red rivulets were beginning to stain the white of his *calzoncillos* [undergarments].

I hurried to the hill-top, to get near enough for a "shot," but the mob, hitherto only scowling, was now openly hostile, and I would have fared ill but for the prompt action of Don Ireneo Chaves, whose reckless bravery is a proverb in all that country of brave men none cared to provoke. With two stanch, well-armed friends, he held back the evil-faced mob, while the instantaneous plates were being snapped at the strange scene below.

Suddenly another fifer came over the hill, followed by more women, and seven Penitentes. Of the latter, four were whipping themselves, and three staggered under crosses of crushing weight. Slowly and solemnly they strode down the slope to the stone-walled graveyard, filed through the roofed entrance, whipped themselves throughout all the paths, knelt in prayer at each grave, kissed the foot of the central board cross, and filed out again. These services lasted twenty minutes. The foremost cross-carrier, after leav-ing the graveyard a few rods behind, fell face down under his fearful load, and lay there with the great cross-arm resting upon his neck. One of the *Hermanos de Luz* ("Brothers of Light," who do not castigate themselves, but act as attendants upon those who do) took a whip and gave him fifty resounding blows on the bare back. Then two *ayudantes* [helpers] lifted him to his feet, laid the great timbers upon his neck, and steadied the ends as he tottered onward. Once he was about to sink again, but they revived him with emphatic kicks. So the ghastly procession crept thrice from morada to campo santo and back.

At seven o'clock that night the fanatic band came marching down to the hospitable house of Colonel Manuel Chaves, the most extraordinary Indian fighter New Mexico ever produced. A little family chapel stands a few rods from the house, behind two sturdy oaks, in whose never-forgotten shade Colonel Chaves rested one awful day fifty-eight years ago, when, sieved by seven Navajo arrows, he was crawling his bloody one hundred and fifty miles homeward to Cebolleta. Hither the procession turned. There were now five *Hermanos Disciplinantes,* but only one of them was using his whip: a short, youthful-seeming fellow of beautiful muscular development. Kneel-ing in turn and kissing the rude cross that leaned against one of the trees,

each one waddled on his knees into the chapel and up to the altar, where all
remained kneeling. Back of them were two-score women on their knees,
while a dozen men stood reverently along the wall. The *Hermano Mayor*
["Senior Brother"], Jose Salazar, a small, amiable-looking shrivel raised his
cracked voice in a hymn, and the audience followed, in the nasal drawl so
dear to native New Mexican singers. It was an impressive sight the little
adobe room, whose flaring candles struggled vainly with the vagrant shadows; the altar bright with chromos [chromolithograph, a colored picture
of the saint] of the saints, a plaster image of the Holy Mother dressed in tulle
[veils] and wreaths of paper flowers; the black-capped, bare-backed
five before the altar and the awe-struck crowd behind as they sang over
and over, with intense feeling "The Columns":

> "Upon a column bound
> Thou'lt find the King of Heaven,
> Wounded and red with blood
> And dragged along the ground.
> In bitter discipline
> If thou would'st ease his pain,
> Draw nigh, O soul, to give
> Peace to the dove divine.
> Alas, Jesus! Alas, my sweet master,
> We long to aid Thee!
> Receive, thou loving power,
> The flowers of this mystery."

Then, at a signal from the Hermano Mayor, the penitent five fell prone
upon their faces, with arms stretched at full length beyond their heads; and
thus they lay, motionless as death, for three-quarters of an hour, while the
singing, with its fife accompaniment, still went on.

The services over, the Penitentes filed over to the house for supper
which dare not be refused them, even in that cultivated Chaves family. The
Hermanos de Luz had already effectually blinded the windows, and the five
active members, filing into the room, locked the door and plugged the
keyhole before they dared remove their head-masks to eat. This care to keep
their identity secret is observed out of a fear for the Church. Still, the sympa-
thizing villagers know pretty surely who each one is.

No one was allowed in the dining-room save the five self-whippers, and
now came my golden opportunity. Metaphorically collaring the Hermano
Mayor, the Hermanos de Luz, and the pitero, I dragged them to my room,
overwhelmed them with cigars and other attentions, showed and gave them
pictures of familiar scenes, and cultivated their good graces in all conceivable
ways. And when the Brothers of the Whip had supped, re-masked themselves
and emerged, the Chief Brother and the Brothers of Light were mine.

On the morning of Good Friday, March 30, I was in the village bright and early; and so was everyone else for twenty miles around. At ten o'clock the Mexican schoolmaster and another prominent citizen started up the canon with me, helping to "pack" my gear. Coming to a point in the road opposite the morada, they sat down, refusing to go nearer, and I had to carry the load alone to a hillock a couple of hundred feet southeast of the house, where I set up the camera.

Soon the procession hove in sight, coming from town. Ahead strode the fifer, proudly fingering his diabolical instrument; then came two hermanos with crosses, and another whipping himself, with half a dozen Hermanos de Luz attending them, then shriveled old Jesus Mirabal reading prayers aloud, and behind him fifty-one women and children, falling down on their knees in the dust-deep road at every fifty feet or so to pray, and singing hymns as they walked between prayers. They bore a large crucifix with the figure of the Redeemer strange to say, dressed in a linen gown a plaster image of the Holy Virgin, and numerous framed chromos of the saints. Tallest among the women was the Mexican wife of the Presbyterian missionary then stationed at San Mateo, a cynical commentary on our mission work.

Reaching the *morada* [building serving a headquarters for the Penitentes] in their deliberate march, the Penitentes laid down their crosses and went inside; the women knelt on the ground before the door and kept up their singing and praying, while the Brothers of Light strode here and there with airs of great responsibility. The ill-faced mob gathered about me, with unpromising looks, and with significant lumps beneath their coats. But just then my lonely guard was relieved by Juan Baca, one of the Hermanos de Luz, who came over from the morada swelled with importance, and whispered most gratifying news. The Hermano Mayor had pondered my request.

After dinner he would hold the procession while I made a picture! So back went the camera into its box, which Juan carried into the morada, and back fell the puzzled mob. Presently the procession was renewed, and I marched beside it to dinner.

Now there were three Brothers using the lash, and two carrying crosses; while two more strode unconcernedly along, each with a burro-load of *entrana* (buckhorn cactus) lashed upon his naked back. The entrana is one of the most depraved of all its diabolical family. Its spines are long, slenderer and sharper than the sharpest needle, yet firm enough to penetrate any ordinary boot. Get one entrana needle into the hide of a steer, and the maddened animal will gallop bellowing over the landscape till it falls from exhaustion. Yet these two fanatics wore huge bundles of it, held on by half-inch hempen ropes drawn so tightly about chest and arms and waist that they cut the skin and stopped the circulation; each must have had thousands of the thorns burrowing into his flesh, but he gave no sign. There was no sham about it. Don Ireneo cut a big entrana antler from beside the road, and threw it upon one of them as he passed. The cruel needles pierced his shoulder so deeply that the heavy branch hung there, yet he never winced nor turned his head! At the foot of Calvary the procession stopped, while the two men with crosses prostrated themselves in the dust the crosses being placed upon their backs and lay thus for ten minutes, the fife and the singers keeping up their discord the while. Every hour of the day these pilgrimages were made between the camposanto and the morada a full third of a mile each way.

Shortly before two o'clock the women returned from town, "making the stations," and halted in front of the morada. Juan Baca brought forth the camera, and the Hermano Mayor marked a spot, about one hundred feet from the door, where I might stand. Then he called the Brothers from the house and formed the procession the cross-bearers in front, then the Brothers of the Whip, and then the Brothers of Light and the women. " 'Sta bueno [Is this good]?" he asked through Juan, and when I replied that it was, he gave orders that no man should stir a finger until the pictures were taken.

This ordeal over, the Penitentes retired again inside the morada, and the women started on a fresh pilgrimage. I was left to chat a moment with Manuel Martin, one of the Brothers of Light, and a remarkable character. He is now said to be over one hundred years old, but is active as a cat. He has a nineteen year-old wife, and frequently walks twenty miles of a morning to visit his father-in-law, who is forty years younger than he, but does not look it. Very diminutive, Manuel is still straight as an arrow, and remarkably strong. They relate in the village that he used to kill a sheep with a single blow of his fist, a great feat for any man. When Manuel lived at Puerto de Luna he was a shepherd, and used to vegetate with his flock a year at a time, on wages of $15 per month. At the end of the year he would return, get his money and spend every cent of it in giving the whole town a grand ball that night!

"And how passes the time?" I asked the old man.

"*Válgame Dios, Señor*," he answered; "but I am not well. I saw a strange and woeful sight last night. One of the Brothers lay sick in the morada, and I was caring for him. At midnight I heard the whistle of Brothers coming from the mountains, and went out. I knelt at meeting them, as is our custom, and when I looked I saw that their feet were bared of flesh nothing but little white bones. Then I looked up, and saw only two skeletons, whipping themselves upon the naked bones of their backs and I ran away, crossing myself. I believe they were Brothers who had broken their vows and now must wander without rest."

Meantime other Hermanos de Luz, including Juan Baca and "Cuate" the cleverest wrestler in the Territory, despite his years had burrowed out a deep hole some fifty feet in front of the morada, and laid the largest cross with its foot at the edge of the hole. The procession of women had returned, and stood solemnly in front of the hundreds of spectators. And now the Hermano Mayor went into the morada with two of his assistants. In a few moments they emerged leading the allotted victim, a stalwart young fellow dressed only in his white drawers and black head-bag. As we learned later, it was Santiago Jaramillo known also as "Santiago Jeems" the cook at the house of Don Roman A. Baca, one of the sheep-kings of the Territory. In his right side was a gaping gash four inches long, from which the blood ran down to the ground in a steady stream. He walked firmly to the prostrate cross, however, and laid himself at full length upon it. A long, new, half-inch rope was brought, and the Hermanos de Luz began to lash him to the great timbers, placing the stiff hemp around his arms, trunk, and legs in three or four loops each, and "cinching up" the slack as un-gently as they would upon a pack-mule. He was sobbing like a child, "Ay! Como estoy deshonrado! Not with a rope! Not with a rope! Nail me! Nail me!" But the Hermano Mayor was obdurate. Always before, up to this very year, the victim had been nailed to the cross by great spikes through hands and feet, and the death of a Penitente during the crucifixion was by no means rare. But the new Hermano Mayor, a more intelligent and humane man than his predecessors, and also perchance with more of the fear of the church before his eyes, drew the line at nails, despite the appeals of the victim not to be dishonored by a lighter agony.

He fared badly enough, as it was. The stiff rope sank deep into his flesh and prohibited the throbbing blood. In less than three minutes his arms and legs were black as a Hottentot's. A clean white sheet was now wound about him from head to foot and tied there, leaving exposed only his purpling arms and muffled head. This was done, so one of the attendants explained to me, that no sharp-eyed bystander might recognize him by scars on his body. Now the rope was knotted to the arms of the cross, so that each end hung free and about thirty feet long. Two stalwart Brothers of Light grasped each end; four others seized the cross; and heavily they lifted it so near to perpendicularity that the lower end dropped into the four-foot hole with an ugly chug! But its living burden made no sign. With shovels and hands the assistants filled in the hole with earth and rocks, and stamped it down, while a stout fellow steadied each guy-rope.

A large rock was next placed five feet from the foot of the cross, and another Penitente in cotton drawers and headbag was led out, with a huge stack of cactus so tightly lashed upon his back that he could not move his hands at all, and scarcely his legs. He lay down with his feet against the cross and his head pillowed upon the stone, while the mass of entrana kept his back sixteen or eighteen inches above the ground. Even this was not a tight enough fit to suit him, and he had a large flat stone brought and crowded under the cactus, so as to press it still more cruelly against his back.

Meantime, in gracious response to my request, the Hermano Mayor had paced off thirty feet from the foot of the cross, that I might come nearer and get a larger picture. And there we stood facing each other, the crucified and I: the one playing with the most wonderful toy of modern progress, the other racked by the most barbarous device of twenty centuries ago.

For thirty-one minutes by the watch the poor wretch upon the cross and he on the bed of thorns kept their places. A deathly hush was upon the crowd. Even the unwilling pito was still. The millstream spilt its music upon the rough old wheel, now locked and unresponsive. The fresh breeze rustled among the piñons on the steep mountainside a few rods away. The undimmed afternoon sun flooded the rugged canon with strange glory.

Across the brook a chubby prairie dog, statuesquely perpendicular, watched the ghastly scene and barked, his creaking disapprobation the only animate sound that reached the ear. Near the cross stood the old Hermano Mayor, and beside him Manuel, Juan, Philomeno, "Cuate," Victorio, Melito. Each had a narrow fillet of wild rose branches bound tightly around his skull. Coming nearer, I saw that the claw-like thorns were forced deep into the skin, and that little crimson beads stood out upon each forehead.

At last the Chief Brother spoke a quiet word. The assistants scooped out the dirt from the hole, lifted the cross from its earthen socket, and laid it upon the ground again. The crucified was relieved of his lashings, was lifted to his feet, and carried to the morada, a stout paisano under each shoulder, while his feet made feeble feint of moving. His brother victim was similarly taken in, and the procession re-formed for its awful pilgrimages, which were kept up till six o'clock. As we walked down the canyon beside the procession, forcibly obliged to stop every time it halted to pray, I had leisure to study the peculiar marching-step of the Penitentes.

The cross bearers stagger as best they may under such fearful burdens, but the whippers have a strange step from which they never vary. Each man stands with his muffled head drooping almost upon his chest, his left hand held upon his right nipple, and his right hand grasping the heavy whip. Shoving his right foot slowly forward to the length of an ordinary step, he plants it with a smart slap, at the same time swinging his right arm upward and backward so that the long, broad lash strikes upon the left side of the back at "the small." Thus he pauses full two seconds, the lash resting upon the raw flesh, then shoves his left foot forward, while bringing his whip back in front of him, and with another stamp swishes the whip over upon the right side of his back. By this time of day their drawers were wet with blood behind to the very ankles. One Hermano de Luz carried a tin-pail containing a decoction of romero [a local wild plant], and every two or three minutes dipped the ends of the "disciplinas" in this, to give them an additional sting.

As we passed Calvary again, a new horror was added. The Hermano Mayor came up behind each of the seven self-torturers, and with a flint knife gashed their backs thrice across , and then "cross-hatched" them thrice up and down. They were no mere scratches, but long, bleeding cuts. This is the official seal of the order, and is annually renewed.

At eight o'clock in the evening the procession came down again from the morada, this time marching the length of the town to hold *tinieblas* (dark services) in the little chapel next to the house of Don Lorenzo Sanchez.

The Penitentes went inside and barred the door on the crowd. There were no lights within, and the windows were carefully shuttered. All that came to the shivering audience outside was the clanking of chains and muffled blows, and groans and shrieks. The services which are intended to represent the arrival of the soul in purgatory lasted an hour.

Then the Penitentes emerged, carrying one of their number in a blanket held by the corners. We learned afterward that he had hugged a stake wrapped with cactus for fifteen minutes, and had succumbed to this fresh torture. Around him plodded seven women, weeping bitterly, but low. Not one but feared it was her own husband. The poor wretch lay long at death's door, but finally recovered.

One short, stocky fellow, who had been particularly zealous in his blows all day, and who had lain upon the thorns at the foot of the cross, attracted my particular attention; and walking back from the chapel to the plaza, a third of a mile, I kept at his side and counted the blows he gave himself two hundred and fifty-one. During the day he had laid on over two thousand; and heaven only knows how many before, but next day he was at work with his irrigating hoe. He is a young man, Antonito Montano by name, and not easy of suppression. A mule once caved in his face, and a soldier in a drunken quarrel gave him grounds for being trepanned; but he is still keen to enjoy such tortures as the most brutal prize-fighter never dreamed of.

At midnight of Good Friday, the Penitentes scattered from the morada toward their homes in some cases forty miles away to meet no more in a religious capacity until another Lent. By their incredible self-torture, one would naturally suppose them to be the most God-fearing and devout of men, but this would be a serious error. There are among them good but deluded men, like the Hermano Mayor, Salazar and Cuate; but many of them are of the lowest and most dangerous class petty larcenists, horse-thieves, and assassins, who by their devotion's during Lent think to expiate the sins of the whole year. The brotherhood, though broken, still holds the balance of political power. No one likes and few dare to offend them; and there have been men of liberal education who have joined them to gain political influence. In fact it is unquestionable that the outlawed order is kept alive in its few remote strongholds by the connivance of wealthy men, who find it convenient to maintain these secret bands for their own ends.

Source: Adapted from "The Penitent Brothers," Charles F. Lummis. *The Land of Poco Tiempo* (New York: Charles Scribner's Sons, 1897), pp. 103–108.

The Living Spectre

One of the common traditional explanations for the return of the dead is that the revenant comes back to fulfill a vow or to accomplish some uncompleted task. In the case of the following narrative, Gil Perez is not a literal revenant, but a "living ghost" ("spectre" or "specter") who, having failed in his duty to protect the Governor of the Philippines, magically reappears in front of another Governor's Palace to redeem himself from his earlier failure.

Apparitions of dead people, *Señor,* of course are numerous and frequent. I myself as on other occasions I have mentioned to you have seen several spectres, and so have various of my friends. But this spectre of which I now am telling you that appeared on the Plaza Mayor at noonday, and was seen by everybody was altogether out of the ordinary: being not in the least a dead person, but a person who wore his own flesh and bones in the usual manner and was alive in them; yet who certainly was walking and talking here on the Plaza Mayor of this City of Mexico in the very self-same moment that he also was walking and talking in a most remote and wholly different part of the world. Therefore in spite of his wearing his own flesh and bones in the usual manner and being alive in them it was certain that he was a spectre: because it was certain that his journeying could have been made only on devils' wings.

The day on which this marvel happened is known most exactly, because it happened on the day after the day that the Governor of the Filipinas [Philippine Islands], Don Gomez Perez Dasmariñas, had his head murderously split open, and died of it, in the Molucca Islands [an archipelago in Indonesia], and that gentleman was killed in that bad manner on the 28th of October in the year 1593. Therefore, since everything concerning this most extraordinary happening is known with so great an accuracy there can be no doubt whatever but that in every particular all that I now am telling you is strictly true.

Because it began in two different places at the same time, it is not easy to say certainly, *Señor,* which end of this story is the beginning of it; but the beginning of it is this: On a day, being the day that I have just named to you, the sentries on guard at the great doors of the Palace and also the people who at that time happened to be walking near by on the Plaza Mayor of a sudden saw an entirely strange sentry pacing his beat before the great doors of the Palace quite in the regular manner: marching back and forth, with his gun on his shoulder; making his turns with a soldierly propriety; saluting correctly those entitled to salutes who passed him; and in every way conducting himself as though he duly had been posted there but making his marchings and his turnings and his salutings with a wondering look on the face of him, and having the air of one who is all bedazzled and bemazed.

What made every one know that he was a stranger in this City was that the uniform which he wore was of a wholly different cut and fabric from that belonging to any regiment at that time quartered here: being, in fact as was perceived by one of the sentries who had served in the Filipinas the uniform worn in Manila by the Palace Guard. He was a man of forty, or thereabouts; well set up and sturdy; and he had the assured carriage even in his bedazzlement and bemazement of an old soldier who had seen much campaigning, and who could take care of himself through any adventure in which he might happen to land. Moreover, his talk when the time came for him to explain himself went with a devil-may-care touch to it that showed him to be a man who even with witches and demons was quite ready to hold his own. His explanation of himself, of course, was not long in coming: because the Captain of the Guard at once was sent for; and when the Captain of the Guard came he asked the stranger sentry most sharply what his name was, and where he came from, and what he was doing on a post to which he had not been assigned.

To these questions the stranger sentry made answer speaking with an easy confidence, and not in the least ruffled by the Captain's sharpness with him that his name was Gil Perez; that he came from the Filipinas, and that what he was doing was his duty as near as he could come to it: because he had been duly detailed to stand sentry that morning before the Governor's Palace and although this was not the Governor's Palace before which he had been posted it certainly was a governor's palace, and that he therefore was doing the best that he could do. And to these very curious statements he added quite casually, as though referring to an ordinary matter of current interest that the Governor of the Filipinas, Don Gomez Perez Dasmarinas, had had his head murderously split open, and was dead of it, in the Molucca Islands the evening before.

Well, Senor, you may fancy what a nest of wasps was let loose when this Gil Perez gave to the Captain of the Guard so incredible an account of himself; and, on top of it, told that the Governor of the Filipinas had been badly killed on the previous evening in islands in the Pacific Ocean thousands and thousands of miles away! It was a matter that the Viceroy himself had to look into. Therefore before the Viceroy who at that time was the good Don Luis de Velasco Gil Perez was brought in a hurry: and to the Viceroy he told over again just the same story, in just the same cool manner, and in just the same words.

Very naturally, the Viceroy put a great many keen questions to him; and to those questions he gave his answers or said plainly that he could not give any answers with the assured air of an old soldier who would not lightly suffer his word to be doubted even by a Viceroy; and who was ready, in dealing with persons of less consequence, to make good his sayings with his fists or with his sword.

In part, his explanation of himself was straightforward and satisfactory. What he told about the regiment to which he belonged was known to be true; and equally known to be true was much of what he told being in accord with the news brought thence by the latest galleon about affairs in the Filipinas. But when it came to explaining the main matter how he had been shifted across the ocean and the earth, and all in a single moment, from his guard-mount before the Governor's Palace in Manila to his guard-mount before the Viceroy's Palace in the City of Mexico, Gil Perez was at a stand. How that strange thing had happened, he said, he knew no more than Don Luis himself knew. All that he could be sure of was that it had happened: because, certainly, only a half hour earlier he had been in Manila; and now, just as certainly, he was in the City of Mexico as his lordship the Viceroy could see plainly with his own eyes. As to the even greater marvel how he knew that on the previous evening the Governor of the Filipinas had had his head murderously split open, and was dead of it, in the Molucca Islands, he said quite freely that he did not in the least know how he knew it. What alone he could be sure of, he said, was that in his heart he did know that Don Gomez had keen killed on the previous evening in that bad manner; and he very stoutly asserted that the truth of what he told would be clear to Don Luis, and to everybody, when the news of the killing of Don Gomez had had time to get to Mexico in the ordinary way.

And then Gil Perez having answered all of the Viceroy's questions which he could answer, and having said all that he had to say stood quite at his ease before the Viceroy: with his feet firmly planted, and his right hand on his hip, and his right arm akimbo and so waited for whatever might happen to be the next turn.

Well, Senor, the one thing of which anybody really could be sure in this amazing matter and of which, of course, everybody was sure was that the devil was at both the bottom and the top of it; and, also, there seemed to be very good ground for believing that Gil Prez was in much closer touch with the devil than any good Christian even though he were an old soldier, and not much in the way of Christianity expected of him had any right to be. Therefore the Viceroy rid himself of an affair that was much the same to him as a basket of nettles by turning Gil Perez over to the Holy Office and off he was carried to Santo Domingo and clapped into one of the strongest cells.

Most men, of course, on finding themselves that way in the clutches of the Inquisition, would have had all the insides of them filled with terror; but Gil Perez, Senor being, as I have mentioned, an old campaigner, took it all as it came along to him and was not one bit disturbed. He said cheerfully that many times in the course of his soldiering he had been in much worse places; and added that—having a good roof over his head, and quite fair rations, and instead of marching and fighting only to sit at his ease and enjoy himself—he really was getting, for once in his life, as much of clear comfort as any old soldier had a right to expect would come his way. Moreover, in his dealings with the Familiars of the Holy Office his conduct was exemplary. He stuck firmly to his assertion that whatever the devil might have had to do with him he never had had anything to do with the devil; he seemed to take a real pleasure in confessing as many of his sins as he conveniently could remember; and in every way that was open to him his conduct was that of quite as good a Christian as any old soldier reasonably could be expected to be.

Therefore while he staid on in his cell very contentedly the Familiars of the Holy Office put their heads together and puzzled and puzzled as to what they should do with him: because it certainly seemed as though the devil, to suit his own devilish purposes, simply had made a convenience of Gil Perez without getting his consent in the matter; and so it did not seem quite fair in the face of his protest that he was as much annoyed as anybody was by what the devil had done with him to put him into a flame-covered *sanbenito* [a garment worn by penitents sentenced to execution by the Spanish Inquisition], and to march him off to be burned for a sorcerer at the next *auto de fe* [Spanish, "act of faith," a euphemism for being burned at the stake]. Therefore, the Familiars of the Holy Office kept on putting their heads together and puzzling and puzzling as to what they should do with him; and Gil Perez kept on enjoying himself in his cell in Santo Domingo and so the months went on and on.

And then, on a day, a new turn was given to the whole matter: when the galleon from the Filipinas arrived at Acapulco and brought with it the proof that every word that Gil Perez had spoken was true. Because the galleon brought the news that Don Gomez Perez Dasmarinas the crew of the ship that he was on having mutinied really had had his head murderously split open, and was dead of it, in the Molucca Islands; and that this bad happening had come to him at the very time that Gil Perez had named. Moreover, one of the military officers who had come from the Filipinas in the galleon, and up from Acapulco to the City of Mexico with the conducta, recognized Gil Perez the moment that he laid eyes on him; and this officer said that he had seen him only a day or two before the galleon's sailing on duty in Manila with the Palace Guard. And so the fact was settled beyond all doubting that Gil Prez had been brought by the devil from Manila to the City of Mexico; and, also, that the devil since only the devil could have done it had put the knowledge of the murderous killing of Don Gomez into his heart. Wherefore the fact that Gil Perez was in league with the devil was clear to all the world.

Then the Familiars of the Holy Office for the last time put their heads together and puzzled and puzzled over the matter; and at the end of their puzzling they decided that Gil Perez was an innocent person, and that he undoubtedly had had criminal relations with the devil and was full of wickedness. Therefore they ordered that, being innocent, he should be set free from his cell in Santo Domingo; and that, being a dangerous character whose influence was corrupting, he should be sent back to Manila in the returning galleon. And that was their decree. Gil Perez, *Señor,* took that disposition of him in the same easygoing way that he had taken all the other dispositions of him, save that he grumbled a little as was to be expected of an old soldier over having to leave his comfortably idle life in his snug quarters and to go again to his fightings and his guard-mounts and his parades. And so back he went to the Filipinas: only his return journey was made in a slow and natural manner aboard the galleon not, as his outward journey had been made, all in a moment on devils' wings.

To my mind, *Señor,* it seems that there is more of this story that ought to be told. For myself, I should like to know why the Familiars of the Holy Office did not deal a little more severely with a case that certainly had the devil at both the bottom and the top of it; and, also, I should like to know what became of Gil Perez when he got back to Manila in the galleon and there had to tell over again about his relations with the devil in order to account for his half-year's absence from duty without leave. But those are matters which I never have heard mentioned; and what I have told you is all that there is to tell.

Source: "The Living Spectre," Thomas A. Janvier. *Legends of the City of Mexico* (New York: Harper & Brothers, 1910), pp. 96–108.

Three Live Witches

The following tales of witchcraft in New Mexico were collected in the last two decades of the nineteenth century. This far-ranging account that includes many specific legends and personal experience narratives provides the primary characteristics of witchcraft as these beliefs developed from the interaction of European and Native American cultures in New Spain and, later, New Mexico Territory: shape-shifting. vindictiveness, and exploitive plotting. For additional information on the Penitentes mentioned below, see "The Penitent Brothers."

If the Puritans had had as much to say about the rest of the vast area now covered by the United States as they did in their narrow New England strip, I should not be writing this. Such witches as they had, they promptly assisted to a more merciful world, but the real home of witchcraft on this continent was as far outside their jurisdiction as their knowledge. No such merciless censors as they were to be found in the arid area which Spain had colonized in the great Southwest long before a Caucasian foot had touched Plymouth Rock; and in the bare, adobe villages which began to dot the green valleys of what is now New Mexico, witchcraft was an institution which none cared to molest. Physically, there were no braver people than these Spanish-speaking pioneers who made the first settlements in the New World. Their whole life was one heroic struggle with wild beasts and wilder men, with suffering, privation, and danger. The colonists of the Atlantic coast, perilous as was their undertaking, had never such gruesome foes as the Spaniards fought here for three centuries. None but brave men would have opened such a wilderness, and none but brave ones could have held it. History records no greater heroisms than the unwritten ones which the rocky mesas of New Mexico witnessed almost daily.

But with all their courage in facing material danger, these simple, uneducated folk shrank from the mysterious and the unknown like children from the dark. During the 40 years that New Mexico has been under our flag, she has changed for the better, but the change is little more than skin-deep. Her sparsely settled area of one hundred and twenty-two thousand square miles holds more that is quaint and wonderful, more of the Dark Ages, more that the civilized world long ago outgrew, than all the rest of the country put together, and today one of the most wonderful things within her bare, brown borders is the survival and prevalence of witchcraft.

There are not now nearly as many witches in New Mexico as there were a few years ago, but there are enough if popular belief is accepted. Of course I am speaking now from the New Mexican standpoint, to which the small, educated class looks back with indulgent incredulity, but in which the common people believe as sincerely as did the Puritans when they burned poor old women at the stake "because they were witches." Of the little Mexican hamlets in the more secluded corners of the Territory, there are few which cannot still boast a resident witch, in whose malignant powers the simple villagers have firmest faith, and the story of whose alleged doings would fill a large volume.

I had the probably unprecedented privilege, a short time ago, of photographing three live witches as they stood in the door of their little adobe house Antonia Morales and Placida Morales, sisters, and Villa, the daughter of Placida, and not more than 17 years old. All three live in the little village of San Rafael, which lies beside the beautiful Gallo Spring in the fertile valley behind that great, black lava-flow which, centuries ago, ran down the valley of the Rio Puerco "Dirty River" from the now extinct craters of the Zuni Mountains. Their house is about in the centre of the straggling village. Only a few hundred feet away stands the little Presbyterian mission schoolhouse, where 30 or 40 Mexican children are learning to read and write, to speak English and "do sums," under the charge of two young ladies from the East. The little church is even closer. But a majority of the people believe more heartily in the witches than they do in the school.

The town is much in awe of these three lone women. No one cares to refuse when they ask for food or other favors. They will do almost anything rather than incur the displeasure of the brujas, as the witches are called. Any one can tell you direful tales of what befell those who were rash enough to offend them. Queer reading these witch stories make in this day and country. Here are some of the remarkable tales which I hear from the believing lips of "the oldest inhabitants."

Francisco Ansures, a good-looking young Mexican, whose adobe house is one of the six that constitute the little village of Cerros Cuates, had the misfortune four years ago to offend one of the witches. I say his misfortune, for he did not know, until the penalty came upon him, that he had offended, and to this day is not aware what particular evil he did to her. But the witch knew, and punished him for his deed, whatever it may have been. She said nothing at the time, but waited patiently till one day she had a chance to give him a cup of coffee. He drank the decoction unsuspectingly. In a few minutes thereafter he was horrified to see that his hair had grown two feet in length, and that his rough overalls had turned to petticoats. Still worse, when he cried out in dismay, his pleasant tenor voice had become a squeaky treble.

In a word, he had been turned into a woman at least, that is what he says, and what his industrious little wife maintains to this day. They declare that he remained a woman for several months, and recovered his proper sex only by paying a male witch who lived in the Canyon de Juan Tafoya to turn him back again.

A witch named Marcelina, a poor, withered little woman about 50 years old, was stoned to death in San Mateo, 30 miles north of San Rafael, in 1887, because she had "turned Don Jose Patricio Marino into a woman, and made Senor Montano very lame."

Montano is still lame; but not nearly so much so as before he helped to kill poor old Marcelina. That pious act not only relieved his feelings, but soothed his distorted muscles also. Marino is again a man and one of very good standing in San Mateo having hired another witch to retransform him into a man's shape.

In the Pueblo Indian town of Zia, less than ten years ago, lived a witch who was quietly but perseveringly causing all the children of the place to die one after the other. At last the people could stand it no longer, and arose in a mass to wipe her out, but found their efforts vain. The priest refused to come from his home in a neighboring town to help them, so they enlisted the sacristan, one of their own number, who had charge of the church. He marched at the head of the mob, carrying a jar of holy water, which he had taken from the church. As they came near, the poor old woman fled, with the mob in howling pursuit. Just as they were about to overtake her, she suddenly turned herself into a dog, and soon distanced them. They got their horses and ran her down; but she changed again to a coyote and ran faster than ever.

It took the riders nearly all day to catch up with her again; and then the coyote became a cat in the twinkling of an eye, and ran up a tall tree. They tried in vain to shake her down; but when the sacristan arrived he threw some holy water up the tree so that it splashed on her, and down she tumbled like a rock, changing back to her human shape as she dropped.

The crowd fell upon her with clubs and hatchets and beat her head and body fearfully, but still she lived and groaned, though any one of her hundred wounds was enough to kill a strong man.

"Untie the knot! Untie the knot!" she kept screaming, and at last a man who was not too infuriated to hear, stooped down and untied a queer little knot which he found in one corner of her blood-soaked blanket. The instant that was loosed her spirit took its flight.

Nicolas Marino, brother of Patricio, once saw a big ball of fire alight in the arroyo which runs through the town of San Mateo. 'Coulas, as he is familiarly called, is a brave man, and though he knew this must be a witch, he started in pursuit. Just as he reached it, the ball of fire turned into a big rat, which ran off through the grass. When he caught up with the rat, it changed to a huge dog, which growled savagely, sprang clear over his head, and disappeared among the willows.

Juana Garcia, a woman of San Mateo, had a daughter named Maria Acacia, who was taken suddenly sick in the evening. As Juana went outside to gather some herbs for medicine, she saw an unknown animal prowling about the house and caught it. No sooner did she get her hands on it than it turned into a woman, whom she recognized as Salia, the witch daughter of Witch Marcelina.

"Cure my daughter," cried Juana, "or I will have you killed!"

Salia promised, and was allowed to go. But when morning came Maria was no better. Juana went straight to Salia's house and demanded, with natural indignation, "Why didn't you cure my daughter, as you promised you would?"

"Pooh! I don't believe she is sick," answered Salia. "We'll go and see."

The witch was a better walker than the mother, and reached the house first. When Juana arrived she found Maria making tortillas cooked on a hot stone. The witch had gone, and the girl was as well as ever.

"What did she do to you?" asked the astonished mother.

"She just took some ashes from the fireplace and rubbed them on my arms, and I got up well," replied Maria.

Juan Baca is one of the best-known characters among the common people in this part of the country. He is a member of the Order of the Penitentes that strange brotherhood of fanatics who whip their bare backs through Lent to expiate the sins of the year, bear huge crosses, fill themselves with the agonizing needles of the cactus, and wind up on Good Friday by crucifying one of their number.

His wife once refused coffee to Salia, who went away angry. Next day a sore formed on Señora Baca's nose, and small, white pebbles kept dropping therefrom. Juan knew what was the matter, and going to Salia's house, he said, "Look, you have bewitched my wife. If you don't cure her at once, I will hang you."

"It is well," answered Salia; "I will cure her."

Juan went home contented. But his wife grew worse instead of better; and taking his long *reata* [lasso], with its easy slipping noose at one end, he went again to Salia's.

"I have come to hang you," said he.

"No, don't! I'll come right over!" cried Salia, and over she went with him. She gave the sick woman a little black powder, and rubbed her nose once. Out came a sinew four inches long, and instantly the nose was as well as ever.

These are only samples. I could tell you a hundred more of the stories implicitly believed by thousands of people in this far-off corner of the United States. Their superstitions as to the general traits of the witches are no less curious and foolish. It is believed that the witches can do anything they wish, but that they never wish to do a good act unless bribed or scared into it. They never injure dumb brutes, but confine their evil spells to human beings who have, knowingly or unwittingly, incurred their wrath.

At night they go flying to the mountains to meet other witches; and hundreds of ignorant people declare that they have seen them sailing through the dark sky like balls of fire. Before leaving home they always exchange their own legs and eyes for those of a dog, cat, or coyote, cry out "*Sin Dios y sin Santa Maria*" which signifies, "Without God and without the Virgin Mary," and then fly off.

Juan Perea, a male witch who died in San Mateo in 1888, once met with a singular misfortune. He had taken the eyes of a cat for one of his nocturnal rambles, leaving his own eyes on the table. During his absence a dog knocked the table over and ate the eyes; and the unlucky witch had to finish his days with the green eyes of a cat. Luckily, the dog did not eat his legs, which were old and tough, or I don't know how he would have got along. Anyone named Juan can catch a witch by going through a curious rigmarole. He draws a large circle on the ground, seats himself inside it, turns his shirt wrong side out, and cries, "In the name of God I call thee, *bruja* [witch]," and straightway whatever witch is near must fall helpless inside his circle. Everyone who lives here can tell you that a Juan has this power, but he seldom uses it, for he knows that if he does so all the witches in the country will fall upon him and beat him mercilessly to death.

Another curious superstition prevalent here is that if you stick a couple of needles into a broom so that they form a little cross, and put it behind the door when a witch is in your house, the witch cannot get out of that door until a dog or a person has passed out ahead. This superstition was employed on one occasion to tease a woman who passed for a witch. Not very long ago, this reputed witch visited the house of some refined and educated Spanish friends of mine in San Mateo, and one of the young ladies made the needle experiment.

The witch started several times to go out, but each time paused at the door for some one else to precede her. All roguishly hung back, and she was there nearly all day. At last a child went out, and the witch rushed out after. Probably she had noticed the trick, and wished to keep up the deceptive reputation of witchcraft.

The sign of the cross, or the spoken name of God or one of the saints, stops a witch at once. I know people here who assert that they were being carried on a witch's back, thousands of miles a minute, to some distant destination; but that when they became alarmed, and cried, "God save me!" they instantly fell hundreds of feet without being hurt and found themselves alone in a great wilderness.

School and church are gradually killing off these strange and childish superstitions, but they die hard, and it will be many a year before New Mexico will be bereft of her last reputed witch.

Source: "Three Live Witches," C. F. Lummis. *A New Mexico David and Other Stories and Sketches of the Southwest* (New York: Charles Scribner's Sons, 1891), pp. 123–133.

The Witch Deer

Legends of supernatural prey and hunters' magic amulets are common cross-culturally. Such tales are more likely to arise in environments in which hunting is not simply a pastime, but a necessity for sustaining life—as was the case in Hispanic New Mexico in the late nineteenth and early twentieth centuries. The following legend of "The Witch Deer" not only expresses the anxiety felt by hunters but substantiates enduring local beliefs in witchcraft and the means of overcoming it.

"Shoo! Scat!" cried Josefa, straightening-up from her work and looking severely at a small brown rogue who had climbed up to the little shelf over the corner fireplace. The adobe floor was spattered with big drops of water, to lay the dust, and Josefa, bent half double to reach it with the short wisp of broom corn which serves in New Mexican homes, was sweeping toward the door the fine gray powder that works up daily from the compact clay.

"Give me that little stone, nana [grandma]." begged the boy. "The one tata [grandpa] carries in his pouch when he goes to hunt."

"Get away, quick, for that is the charm of the Magic Deer! Much care! For if ever thou touch that, thy grandfather will see to thee!"

Anastacio clambered down reluctantly from the old chair, and went outside to play with the burro. But the stone weighed on his mind. It was a very ordinary-looking pebble, gray, light, porous, and without any particular shape looking, in fact, like one of the pieces of pumice which were so common in the mountains. But somehow it had a fascination for Anastacio. And that evening, when we all sat by the crackling fire, he climbed on his grandfather's knee and said, "Go, tata, tell me what is this stone of the Magic Deer, that I may not play with it."

"To play with that?" exclaimed Don Jose, in a tone of horror. "Child! That little stone is very precious. For no other hunter in New Mexico has the like, and if it were lost or broken, we should be ruined, since only with it is it possible to kill the deer which are enchanted, as are many. And to get that stone I passed a sad time."

"How? Where? When? With the Enchanted Deer? Tell me, tatita!"

"Yes, with the *Venado Encantado* [Enchanted Deer], and in many ways." And Don Jose, the luckiest hunter in Rio Arriba, a gray-headed but sharp-eyed Mexican whom I count a staunch friend and a brave man, even if he does believe some things I do not nodded to me, as if for permission to tell the story.

I had often heard of the Witch Deer, and knew that a very large proportion of the natives of New Mexico believe firmly in this and in many other forms of witchcraft. I knew, too, that Don Jose was a scrupulously truthful man. The years of our acquaintance had proved that beyond doubt. Whatever in his story might be supernatural would have to be charged to his faith, and not to any intention of deceiving.

"You must know, Don Carlos," said he, "that while there are many witches here, there is one kind that delights most to vex hunters. Without doubt you also will have seen the Enchanted Deer, as much as you hunt."

"No," I answered. "I have never seen one, but I have heard of them all over New Mexico these five years."

"Sure! For there are many; and many have lost their lives thereby, for the Witch Deer is more dangerous than bear or mountain lion. Only when one has the stone which they wear in the first fork of their horns is it possible to conquer them, for that makes one not to be seen."

"But I can see you, Don Jose," I interrupted, smiling, as he held up the magic stone.

"But, friend, that is different! For it is only in its use. Now I want you to see me; but when I carry this no deer in the sierra has eyes for me, and I could walk even up to them, taking care only that they scented me not."

It is worse than useless to argue against these beliefs. Don Jose would never be convinced, and the incredulity of a friend could only hurt his feelings, and, besides being ill-mannered, further caviling would lose me a story, so I said, simply, "All right, *compadre,* tell us all about it."

Well, then, thus it was, and you shall see I am right. It makes many years now, for it was long before I married me with Josefa, in the year of [18]67. Her father was Alcalde of Abiquiu [a small town in northern New Mexico]. I loved my parents also. When I was a young man, already grown, strong as you may yet see and well taught in the ways of hunting, I came often to these mountains for game; and our house was never without dried meat in plenty. There was one that hunted with me, and they always called him *Cabezudo,* because of his strong head; but in truth he was Luis Delgado, a cousin of me. In heart we were as brothers, and either would give his life for the other. Often the old men of Abiquiu told us of the Witch Deer, which could never be killed unless by a hunter unseen; and Luis answered always: "Aha! When there is a deer too strong for this rifle, let him eat me!" For, you see, he believed not in witches. This was the only thing we ever quarreled about that he was without faith.

"It came that in October of the year [18]60 we were together camped in the Valles, and with much care, since the Navajos were bad. We had a house of logs, very strong, and in it already was a wonder of dried meat of deer and bear. We went forth always together, for fear of the Indians, but by good luck they molested us not. As for game, I think there was never such a year.

"One day, when the first snow was three hours old, we came to a round mesa that stood on the plateau, and near the foot of it were tracks of a deer. But alas! I knew then that it was no true deer, for its foot prints were great as those of a horse. It will be the Venado Encantado, said I to Luis. Let us go the other way! But he said: "What Enchanted Deer, nor yet what mouse-traps? Get out! I thought thee a man! Thou that only yesterday didst kill, with dagger alone, the great she-bear, and now wouldst run from a deer track! And it was true; for since the bear, we had wounded, was upon us before there was room to reload, I had the luck to dispose of her with my hunting-knife."

"Wrong of me it was, but I had shame at the words of Luis, and followed him. 'Truly this is grandfather of all the deer!' he cried. 'For never have I seen such tracks. And his horns we will take to Abiquiu, though they shall weigh like a tree. Come on!' "

"With that we pursued the tracks, wondering always at their greatness. They went a little around the foot of the mesa, and then up a steep way to its top. When we came to the top, where was a cleft in the rocks, so that one could get up, we found a large level place, round, and with a rim of cliffs below, so that nowhere else was it possible to reach the summit. The trail went away among the junipers, and we followed it cautiously, knowing that the deer must be here, since no tracks led down.

And of a sudden, crawling around a clump of trees, we stood before him. Ay, senor! How great he was! Great as a tall horse, and upon his head the keys [horns] were as the branches of a blasted cedar. There he stood, a thing of fifty yards away, looking at us with his head high, as if mocking. My heart forgot its count; for truly he was nothing of this earth that beast with a look so cunning—and so terrible.

"What a beast! Luis whispered. At the throat, to break his neck. But save thou thy fire, for in case and putting his rifle firm as a rock, he fired. But as the smoke blew by, there stood the deer, wagging his head scornfully, for the bullet had rebounded from him. So it is with these beasts that are witches, for when they see you, no ball will enter their hide. And then, putting down his head till that the horns lacked but a foot from the ground, he came like a large rock leaping down the mountain.

"Now I knew well that he was no mortal thing, and that I had no right to shoot. But for sake of Luis, who was pouring new powder in his rifle, I cared not even if I should be accursed; and when the beast was very close I sprang to one side and gave him the ball, of an ounce weight, squarely upon the side. But it could not enter him. Luis jumped, too, and the brute passed between us like a strong wind. In a moment he turned and charged us again, and I am sure I saw smoke come from his nose. As for his eyes, they were pure fire. Run for yourself! cried Luis, and he made for the tree, while I took the other way. Turning at a juniper, I ran for the edge of the cliff; but just as I came there, there was a scream, and looking across my shoulder, I saw the deer making with his horns as one does with his spade upon hard ground.

"After that I could go no more to our camp, but came straightway to Abiquiu. When they heard what had been, all the town mourned for Luis was well beloved. But none were surprised, for they said, 'Always we told him of the Venado Encantado, but he would not believe. And now it has come true. Poor headstrong Luis!' "

"As for me, I sickened, and was much time in bed. And always I saw the deer leaping upon Luis and tearing him, until it was not to be borne. When at last I was cured, I could think only to kill the Witch Deer, and avenge my poor *compañero*. I asked of all the old men if there was a way how to do it; but all said, Beware, lest he trample thee also! And Josefa prayed me to think no more of it, for she would never marry one who put himself against the witches. I know not how, Don Carlos, for I too feared, but Luis would not let me rest.

"Twice I went alone to the mesa, for no one would companion me. There was always the deer; but I kept under the rocks, where he could not reach me, and waited my turn. Once, when my aim was true upon his heart, the rifle only snapped; and when I went to prime with double care, the flint was all in cracks, so that it would not strike a spark. And again, when I shot him between the very eyes, from near, it did him nothing. So I saw it was useless.

"From then all went ill. Even the wild turkeys had no fear of me, for I could shoot nothing. And in Abiquiu I was mocked, for the young men had been jealous that formerly I had killed more game than any, and now they taunted me for the starved hunter.

"At the last I thought of one who lived in the canyon, of Juan Tafoya a witch, they say, very wise in such things and to him I went. When he had heard my story, he said: 'But, man! knowest thou not that this is the Venado Encantado? How dost thou think to kill him? For he has in his horns a stone of great power, having the which he cannot be harmed. There is only one way in which it could be done, and that is to shoot him when he sees thee not. But that, even the best hunter cannot do, for the animal is very wise and of sharp sight. Only having an invisible stone could one do it.

"And have other deer this stone? I asked; and he replied, "There are some, for this is not the only Witch Deer. But none of them canst thou kill if they see thee."

"After that they saw me little in Abiquiu, for I was always hunting. For many months I pursued the trail of every buck deer, killing many. And at last, shooting from ambush one that passed me unsuspecting, I found in the first fork of its horns a stone like this, but not the half of it in size. This I proved in many ways, and clear it was that now my luck had changed.

"Being satisfied of this, then, I loaded my rifle with great pains, and went one evening in search of the Venado Encantado. Coming to the mesa by night, I camped among the rocks, without a fire, and in the morning, before the sun, climbed up without a little noise. In my pouch was the stone, and my rifle was well ready. When I came through the cleft at the top, there stood the deer, looking straight at me, not twenty yards distant, and I threw my rifle to my shoulder, giving myself up for lost. But he moved not, and watching him, I perceived that he did not see me at all the which is proof that the stone makes one to be invisible.

At this I took heart, and with a true aim on his throat, fired. He leaped thus high in the air and fell dead, and coming to him, I found that the ball had broken his neck.

"His meat I did not touch, for besides being accursed, he had killed my Luis, whose bones I brought away to Christian ground in Abiquiu. But in the first fork of the horns, which were taller than my head, I found this stone which you see. Since I have that, I kill whatsoever deer with ease, because they cannot see me. What think you, then?"

We sat for a few moments silent, watching the flames that licked and twisted about the cedar sticks in the fireplace. Anastacio was voiceless, with an awe too strong even for his boyish excitement; and as for me, the story of Luis's death had brought back some vivid and uncanny memories. But Don Jose, who really cared enough for me to wish to lead me out of the darkness of error, followed the matter up.

"Do you not see, Don Carlos, that there are Witch Deer? For look at his fierceness, and that he could not be hurt until I had a charm-stone like his own. And you know that I tell you truth."

"Yes, old fellow, I know you tell me the truth as you see it. But it is nothing strange for a buck to be bravo in the fall that I myself have suffered by. And I fancy you could have killed him before, if you had not felt so sure that you couldn't."

Then I was rather ashamed to have said even so much, and as gently as it could be said, for I do not admire the always superior person. But the old man understood, and was not offended; only he shook his head with real sadness, and said, "Ah, that way was Luis. God keep you from being taught as he was!"

Source: "The Witch Deer," Charles F. Lummis. *The Enchanted Burro And Other Stories as I Have Known Them From Maine to Chile and California* (Chicago: A. C. McClurg & Co., 1912), pp. 85–99.

Witch Tales from New Mexico

The following set of local legends validate and explain beliefs in witch-craft that have been held in traditional Latino communities of New Mexico. The beliefs owe their origins to both Native American and European supernatural folklore.

BECOMING A WITCH

In New Mexico it is believed that *Los brujos* (male witches) or *brujas* (female witches) are mischievous individuals who practice evil on their neighbors, often for little or no cause. Generally, however, it is on their enemies that witches practice the evil doings which they are able to perform. No one is born a witch. Witchcraft is a science, a kind of learning which may be learned from other witches. Near Pena Blanca, in central New Mexico, there is said to be a school of witches. The apprentice first enters their cave, where the Devil and old witches preside. At first the beginner is taught to transform herself into a dove, then into an owl, and finally into a dog. Anyone who is a witch can give his or her powers to another one; though an individual, by practicing evil, may, on agreement with the Devil, become a witch. New Mexicans speak of a witch as being in agreement with the Devil (*pactado con el diablo* or *pautau con el diablo*).

People, young and old, have a terrible fear of witches and their evil doings. Numerous stories cling around their beliefs. The means of doing harm which the witches have at their disposal are various, but in practically all their methods they bring into play their power of being transformed into any animal whatsoever.

THE WITCH WHO REMOVED HER EYES

A lady once visited with a lady friend whom she did not know to be a witch. Both retired in the evening and went to sleep in the same bed. About midnight (the hour when witches go forth from their homes to practice mischief and take revenge on their enemies) the visitor saw her friend get up from the bed and light a candle. Presently she produced a large dish, placed it on a table, pulled out both of her eyes, and, putting them in the dish, flew out through the chimney, riding on a broomstick. The visitor could no longer stay in the house of the witch, but dressed in haste and ran to her home.

THE WOUNDED WITCH

The owl, called in New Mexico *tecolote*, is very much feared, and is supposed to be the animal whose form the witches prefer to take. The hoot of the owl is an evil omen; and the continuous presence of an owl at nightfall near any house is a sure sign that witches are approaching with evil intentions, or that some evil is about to visit the house.

In a certain village in northern New Mexico, which was considered a favorite rendezvous for witches, a certain house had been surrounded for various nights by owls and foxes (the fox is another animal whose form witches like to take). Fearing harm from witches, since the hooting of the owls and the howling of the foxes had become almost insufferable, men went out to meet them with bows and arrows. The owls and foxes disappeared in all directions, with the exception of one old fox, which had been wounded near the heart by an arrow. No one dared to approach the wounded fox, however; and the next morning it was discovered that an old lady, a witch, living near by, was in her deathbed, with an arrow-wound near the heart.

FOX WITCH

On another occasion a man was riding on a fast horse and saw a fox. He started in pursuit; and after a long chase, when the fox was very tired and was already dragging its tongue along the ground, a sudden transformation took place. At a sharp turn of the road the fox stopped, and the rider did the same. To his amazement, he at once perceived a gray-haired woman sitting on a stone and panting in a terrible manner. Recognizing in her an old woman who was his neighbor, and whom he had suspected of being a witch, he went his way and troubled her no more.

BEWITCHMENT

A witch may have a person under the influence of some evil, illness, or even vice, at will. The unfortunate individual who is beset by witches is also pursued and molested by devils and other evil spirits who help the witches. The general name for any evil or harm caused by a witch is, in New Mexico, *maleficio* ("spell, enchantment, harm"), and the verb is *maleficiar* ("to do harm, to bewitch"). *Estar maleficiau* ("to be under the spell or influence of a witch") is the greatest of evils, and hard to overcome.

A witch, however, may be compelled by physical torture to raise the spell or cease doing harm; but this method is not advisable, since sooner or later the witch will again take revenge. In some instances, it is said, innocent old women have been cruelly tortured in attempting to force them to cure imaginary or other wrongs of which they were accused.

On one occasion a witch was roped and dragged until she restored health to one she had *maleficiau.* One of the more common evils which witches cause is madness or insanity; and the person may be restored, as a rule, by causing the witch to endure great physical pain. All kinds of physical ills are said to be caused by witches.

A certain woman suffered great pain in the stomach, and it was feared that she was *maleficiada.* Some living creature was felt to move about within her stomach; and her relatives became alarmed, and attributed the trouble to an old woman who was suspected of being a witch. She was purposely called in to visit the sick one as *a curandera* ("popular doctor"); and, fearing violence, she approached the *maleficiada* and instantly caused a large owl—the cause of her illness—to come out of her stomach.

WITCH'S CONFESSION

The *brujas* (generally women) are women who are wicked *(pautadas con el diablo)* and non-Christian. By confessing their sins to a priest, repenting, and abandoning their devilish ways, they may become good Christian women. A certain witch desired to forsake her evil ways and save her soul, since those who die witches cannot expect salvation. She confessed to a priest, and gave him a large bundle in the shape of a ball, which consisted largely of old rags, and pins stuck into it, the source and cause of her evil powers. The priest took the diabolical bundle and threw it into a fire, where, after bounding and rebounding for several minutes in an infernal manner, it was consumed, and the compact with the Devil ceased *(ya no estaba pautada con el diablo).*

Source: Adapted from "New-Mexican Spanish Folk-Lore," Aurelio M. Espinosa. *Journal of American Folklore* 23 (1910): 395–418.

Select Bibliography

Bierhorst, John. *Latin American Folktales: Stories from Hispanic and Indian Traditions.* New York: Knopf Publishing, 2001.

Campa, Arthur L. *Hispanic Culture in the Southwest.* Norman: University of Oklahoma Press, 1979.

Castro, Rafaela G. *Chicano Folklore: A Guide to the Folktales, Traditions, Rituals and Religious Practices of Mexican Americans.* New York: Oxford University Press, 2001.

Griego y Maestas, José, and Rudolfo Anaya. *Cuentos: Tales from the Hispanic Southwest.* Santa Fe: The Museum of Santa Fe Press, 1980.

Simmons, Marc. *Coronado's Land: Essays on Daily Life in Colonial New Mexico.* Albuquerque: University of New Mexico Press, 1991.

Toor, Frances. *A Treasury of Mexican Folkways: The Customs, Myths, Folklore, Traditions, Beliefs, Fiestas, Dances, Songs of the Mexican People.* New York: Random House, 1985.

Villarino, José Pepe, and Arturo Ramírez. *Aztlán, Chicano Culture and Folklore: An Anthology.* New York: McGraw-Hill, 1998.

Weigle, Marta, and Peter White. *The Lore of New Mexico.* Albuquerque: University of New Mexico Press, 1988.

West, John O. *Mexican-American Folklore.* Atlanta: August House, 1988.

Index

activists, Chicano, 3
Adam, 9–10
alligator, in Latin culture, 62–63
American, on becoming, 17–20
animals in culture: alligator, 62–63;
    ant, 121–23; bear, 52–56; birds, 9,
    65, 166; cockroach, 63; coyote, 59–
    66, 67–69, 70–74, 121; crow, 40–
    44; deer, 160–64; dog, 64, 121–23;
    eagle, 121–23; fish, 9; fox, 70–74,
    108–10, 166; hen, 63–64; jaguar,
    34; lion, 40–41, 64, 67–69, 121–23;
    mazacuata, 10; owls, 166; quetzal,
    9; rabbit, 23–27, 57–66, 67–69;
    rooster, 65; snake, 9, 10, 64–65;
    steer, 65; tiger, 34–38; worms,
    108–10
ant, in Latin culture, 121–23
anti-Semitism, 7–10
Apache, 29
Apodaca, Pablo, 80–84
apparitions, 150–54. *See also*
    supernatural
Armijo, Juan, 92–93
Aztec Empire, 115–17

Baca, Elfego, 99–103
Baca, Juan, 145–46, 158
Baker, Frank, 91–92
Bakers, Robert, 95
Barber, Charley, 92–94, 96
bear, in Latin culture, 52–56
Beauty and the Beast tale, 52–56
bewitchment, 166–67
Billy the Kid, 91–98

birds, in Latin culture, 9, 65, 166
Bluebeard, 57–58
Bonney, William H. *See* Billy the Kid
Brown Power movement, 3
brujas (female witches), 156, 165, 167.
    See also witchcraft
brujos (male witches), 165. *See also*
    witchcraft
buckhorn cactus, penitents and,
    145–46
buffalo hunters, 87–90
Bullet-Swallower, 127–32
buried treasure, manuscripts on,
    12–16

Cabeza de Vaca, Alvar Nunez, vii,
    11–12
cacao, 8
Central American folktales, 7–10
Chacon, Fernando, 13–16
Chaves, Ireneo, 143
Chaves, Jose, 92–93, 94, 95
Chaves, Manuel, 143–44
Chicano activists, 3
children, parents and, 23–27, 40–44,
    45–47, 108–10, 124–26
Chilean folktales, 45–47
Christianity, witchcraft and, 167
Christian narrative, 7–10
Christian traditions: death, 127–32;
    exorcism, 133–38; marriage, 52–56,
    127–32; saints' images, 139–40
Cihuacoatl, 124
Cinderella tale, 45–47
Coatepec, 4

cockroach, in Latin culture, 63
cofradias, 8–9
Comanche, 14–16, 18, 29
conflict, 87–112; political, 17–20
Conquistadores, Spanish, 115, 117
Cordova, Gabriel A., 57, 118
Cordova, Lazaro, 100–101
Coronado, Francisco Vasquez de, 12
Cortés, Hernan, 115
coyote, in Latin culture, 59–66, 67–69, 70–74, 121
Cozcaapa, fountain of, 6
Crichton, Kyle, 101
cross, sign of the, 159
crow, in Latin culture, 40–44

Dasmarifias, Gomez Perez, 150–54
dead, return of, 150–54
death, Christian tradition and, 127–32
De Castro, Bernardo, 11–16
deer, in Latin culture, 160–64
Devil, 53, 133–38, 152–54. See also evil; witchcraft
dog, in Latin culture, 64, 121–23
dragon-slayer, 80–84

eagle, in Latin culture, 121–23
El Dorado, 11
El Señor Milagroso, 139–40
evil: characters, 3–6, 48–51, 56–57, 105–7, 119, 121–23; deeds, 65–66, 105, 156–57. See also Devil; witchcraft
exorcism, Christian tradition of, 133–38

fairies, 104–5
females: as bogey figures, 124–26; as heroines, 23–27, 40–44, 52–56, 108–10; victimization of, 57–58
Ferguson, Harvey, 101
fish, in Latin culture, 9
fools, 59–66, 67–69, 70–74
fox, in Latin culture, 70–74, 108–10, 166
French, Jim. See White, Jim French
Frisco Affair, 99–103

Gallegos, Guadalupe (Lupita), on becoming an American, 17–20
Gallegos, Lucas, 91
Garrett, Pat, 96, 97
ghosts, living, 150–54
Goliath of Gath, 28
Gran Quivira, 12
greed, punishment for, 104–7

Hamilton, George, 94
hen, in Latin culture, 63–64
Hermanos de Luz (Brothers of Light), 143–49
Hermanos Disciplinantes, 143–44
heroes, 143–44; Apodaca, Pablo, 80–84; John Tiger as, 34–38; Montoya, Lucario as, 28–33; parental abuse and, 23–27
heroines, 124; abused women and, 57–58; Beauty and the Beast tale, 52–56; Cinderella tale, 45–47; Snow White tale, 48–51; witches and, 52–56
Holy Office, 134–38, 152–54
hound, in Latin culture, 121–23
Huehuequauhtitlan (Old Quauhtitlan), 6
Huitzilopochtli, 3–6
human as trickster, 75–79
hunting, 160–64

Impress of the Hands, 6
infanticide, 124–26
Inquisition, Spanish, 133–38, 152–54

jaguar, in Latin culture, 34
Jesus, 7–10
John Tiger, 34–38

Kimbrall, George, 95–96
Kiowa, 89–90

La Malinche, 124
Lent, as season of Penitent activity, 141–49, 158
Leon, Ponce de, 11
Lincoln County War, 91–98
lion, in Latin culture, 40–41, 64, 67–69, 121–23

Los Hermanos Penitentes (the Penitent Brothers), 141–49
Lummis, Charles F., 11, 16, 28, 84, 149, 159, 164

Macky, Pedro, 97–98
magic, 118–20, 121–23, 160–64. *See also* supernatural
Manzano Gang, 100–102
Marfes, 91, 93, 94–95, 96
marriage, 24–27, 39–42, 52–56, 60–62, 127–32
Martinez, Atanasio, 92
mazacuata (snake), in Latin culture, 10
McCarty, William Henry. *See* Billy the Kid
Mexican folktales, 48–51, 59–66, 115–17, 121–23, 124–26, 133–38
Milton, John, 94
Montezuma, 11
Montezuma II, 115–17
Montoya, Lucario, 28–33
moon, in folktales, 25–26
Moors, prejudice against, 108–9, 133–35
Mote, Billy, 91–92, 97

Nahua cultures, 3
Nane, Macky, 92
Native Americans: Apache, 29; Comanche, 14–16, 18, 29–32; Kiowa, 89–90; Navajo, 28, 29; Piute, 29; Pueblos, 29; Uncompahgres, 29; Ute, 28–32; Yaqui, 44
Navajo, 28, 29
necromancers, 3–6
Negro, 40
New Mexico folktales, 17–20, 28–33, 80–84, 91–103, 141–49, 155–67

ogres, 105–7, 121–23
Old Quauhtitlan, 6
Order of the Penitents, 141–49, 158
origins: on American, becoming, 17–20; anti-Semitism, 7–10; Aztec, 3–6; Jesus, 7–10; Quetzalcoatl, 3–6; Tezcatlipoca, 3–6

Ortega, Alvino, 87–88
Ortega, Jesus Maria, 87–88
outlaws, 87–90
owls, in Latin culture, 166

Papantzin (Princess), 115–17
parents, children and, 23–27, 40–44, 45–47, 108–10, 124–26
patterns of three, influence of, 23–27, 40–44
Penitentes, 141–49, 158
Perez, Gil, 151–54
Piute, 29
Pueblos, 29

Quauhtitlan, 5–6
quetzal, (birds) in Latin culture, 9
Quetzalcoatl, 3–6

rabbit, in Latin culture, 23–27, 57–66, 67–69
race relations, 17–20
religion: corruption in, 48–51; marriage and, 52–56; Roman Catholicism, 48–51, 52–56, 127–32
Romero, Juan Jesus, 87
Romero, Juan Policarpio, 87, 90
rooster, in Latin culture, 65

saints' images as Christian tradition, 139–40
Salcedo, Nemecio, 15–16
Satan. *See* Devil
Scroggin, John, 92
self-flagellation, 141–49, 158
Seven Cities of Cibola, 11–12
shape-shifting, 155–59, 166
snake, in Latin culture, 9, 10, 64–65
Snow White tale, 48–51
society: buffalo hunters, 87–90; class differences, 111–12; family life, 17–20; Frisco Affair, 99–103; greed in, 104–7; outlaws, 91–103; sacrifice, 108–10
sorcerers, 108–10. *See also* supernatural
Southwest folktales, 34–44, 48–51, 87–90, 121–23; greed, punishment

for, 104–7; human as trickster, 75–
    79; treasure tale, 11–16
Spanish Conquistadores, 115, 117
Spanish exploration, vii
Spanish Inquisition, 133–38, 152–54
Spanish manuscripts on buried
    treasure, 12–16
specters, 150–54
spells, removing, 166–67
steer, in Latin culture, 65
sun, in folktales, 26
supernatural, 34–38, 113–67; dead,
    return of, 150–54; fairies, 104–5;
    females, as bogey figures, 124–26;
    living ghosts, 150–54; Montezuma
    II and, 115–17; necromancers, 3–6;
    ogres, 105–7, 121–23; *Penitentes*,
    141–49; prey, 160–64; Princess
    Papantzin and, 115–17; saints'
    images, 139–40; shape-shifting,
    155–59, 166; specters, 150–54;
    Traga-Balas, Antonio, 127–32;
    transformation, 121–23; wailing
    woman, 124–26; witchcraft, 52–56,
    118–20, 137, 142, 151, 160–67. *See
    also* Devil; magic; witchcraft
superstition, 133–38, 139–40, 155–59,
    160–64
Swin, Macky, 92–95

Tar Baby, 59–66
Tempacpalco, 6
Tequiua, 5
Tezcatlipoca, 3–6
tiger, in Latin culture, 34–38
Titlacahuan, 3–6
Tlacahuepan, 3–6

Tollan, 3–6
Toltecs, 3–6
Toueyo, 4
Traga-Balas, Antonio, 127–32
transformation, 121–23
treasure tale, 5–6, 11–16
tricksters: coyote as, 59–66, 67–69;
    fox as, 70–74; human as, 75–79;
    rabbit as, 59–66
Trujillo, Francisco, 91–98
Trujillo, Juan, 91

Uemac, 4
Ugalde, Juan de, 13
Uncompahgres, 29
Urdemalas, Pedro de, 75–79
Ute, 28–32

vaca de lumbre, 124
Vasques, Manuel Jesus, 87–90
villains, 75–79

wailing woman, 124–26
Water of Precious Stones, 6
White, Jim French, 94
White Flower, 48–51
Wilson, Charley, 97
wind, in folktales, 26
witchcraft, 118–20, 137, 142, 151,
    160–67; Beauty and the Beast tale,
    52–56; shape-shifting, 155–59. *See
    also* Devil; evil
Witch Deer, 160–64
witches. *See* witchcraft
worms, in Latin culture, 108–10

Yaqui, 44

About the Author

THOMAS A. GREEN is Associate Professor of Anthropology at Texas A&M University. His many books include *The Greenwood Library of American Folktales* (2006) and *The Greenwood Library of World Folktales* (2008).